Once you delve into the pages of this book you'll quickly discover that a powerful anointing and hunger for more of the Holy Spirit will fall on you. Katherine introduces us to Holy Spirit in a new, fresh dimension. Whether you are a new believer or have been Spirit-empowered for many years, you will encounter Him in a powerful way as you take in the words written here.

—CINDY JACOBS
GENERALS INTERNATIONAL

Imagine what your life would be like if you were a true friend to the Holy Spirit of God. *Life With the Holy Spirit* will give you amazing insights on how to be fully encouraged, fully embraced, and fully empowered in your relationship with God. Katherine Ruonala has given us another masterpiece. In this, her third, book you will uncover some glorious secrets about the Holy Spirit and what it means to become a friend of God. We found such delightful truths shining from the pages of this book! *Life With the Holy Spirit* may be the most pleasant surprise you've had in a long while. Read it from cover to cover, and let the Holy Spirit come upon you!

—BRIAN AND CANDICE SIMMONS
STAIRWAY MINISTRIES AND THE PASSION TRANSLATION
PROJECT

Life With the Holy Spirit emboldens readers to develop their personal relationship with the Holy Spirit by way of expounding scriptural truths and presenting personal testimonies. Whether someone is beginning his journey as a Christ follower or has walked with Jesus for years, this book is sure to propel him into a deeper relationship with the Trinity, especially the Holy Spirit. He doesn't just work through you; He partners with you!

—GABE AHN
SENIOR PASTOR, EXECUTIVE PRODUCER, HROCK CHURCH
PASADENA, CALIFORNIA

In a culture that has seen the Holy Spirit marginalized, misrepresented, or even ignored, Katherine Ruonala calls for our return to a fresh awareness of the Spirit's work in our lives. In these pages we see the beauty of simultaneously receiving and pursuing His fullness. Life in the Spirit is like a beautiful dance. He leads, and we follow. Katherine helps us see how to live this out practically. I love this book!

—STEPHEN CHITTY
LEAD PASTOR, CHRISTIAN LIFE CHURCH AND SOUTH
CAROLINA SCHOOL OF LEADERSHIP

As a new believer I had the high privilege of meeting and being interviewed by Kathryn Kuhlman. She had the highest miracle ministry I have ever seen. But her secrets of intimacy with the Holy Spirit went with her to the grave. Katherine Ruonala has that same intimacy with the Holy Spirit and is entering into that same miracle anointing! In this book she equips you to walk in that special communion with the Holy Spirit and in power. Welcome to the greatest adventure of your life. The Holy Spirit is calling you!

—SID ROTH
HOST, *IT'S SUPERNATURAL!*

Before every major historic revival in history you can trace back to a group of people who started to get to know the third person of the Trinity, the Holy Spirit. Katherine has written an amazing book that will introduce you to a deeper life in God because you will know the marvelous friend of heaven, the Spirit of God! He plays such an essential role, but He is treated like an *it* and a secondary character in the great biblical message. When we place Him in our hearts as the One who gives us full access to our connection to the rest of the Trinity, we start to develop an understanding of how to walk with God the way Jesus prayed in John 17:24: Father, I desire for them to be one as We are one. *Life With the Holy Spirit* is a divine setup for your life. You need to know how this mysterious person of God moves in your life so that you can have true partnership with His plans and desires for you and the world around you!

—Shawn Bolz
Best-Selling Author, *Translating God, Growing Up With God*, and *Keys to Heaven's Economy*
www.bolzministries.com

Katherine Ruonala's personal and powerful relationship with the Holy Spirit casts the shadow of Jesus Christ across the globe today. She believes all things are possible, and she teaches you how you can do the same. Want to fellowship with the Holy Spirit? Want to walk in the fruit, gifts, and conviction of the Holy Spirit? *Life With the Holy Spirit* will inspire you to do just that!

—James W. Goll
Cofounder, Encounters Network
Founder, God Encounters Training
Best-Selling Author, International Speaker, Life-Language Trainer

The greatest prayer of my life is that I want everyone in the world to experience a God who looks like Jesus. Katherine

Ruonala is a friend, but more importantly she is a friend of the Holy Spirit. The presence, person, priority, purpose, and power of the Holy Spirit are in her and on her life and ministry. Within *Life With the Holy Spirit* is an invitation to move from an ordinary to an extraordinary lifestyle that will change the world. I encourage you to read it.

—LEIF HETLAND
FOUNDER AND PRESIDENT, GLOBAL MISSION AWARENESS
AUTHOR, *SEEING THROUGH HEAVEN'S EYES* AND *HEALING THE ORPHAN SPIRIT*

I love this book! *Life With the Holy Spirit* empowers believers to take off the limitations and to live out of their God-created identity as they pursue new depths of intimacy with the Trinity. This book is a catalyst for revival and reformation by launching ordinary believers into a life of the extraordinary! In the pages of this book you will discover relational principles that will empower you to partner with the Holy Spirit and enable you to live in the miraculous as you step into your God-created identity and fulfill your destiny! If you are longing to experience a genuine encounter with the supernatural love, power, presence, and fellowship of the Holy Spirit in your life, *Life With the Holy Spirit* is a must-read!

—TONY THOMPSON
SENIOR PASTOR, GLORY CITY CHURCH ATLANTA
FOUNDER, TONY THOMPSON MINISTRIES

LIFE WITH

the

Holy

Spirit

LIFE WITH
the
Holy
Spirit

Katherine Ruonala

CHARISMA
HOUSE

Most CHARISMA HOUSE BOOK GROUP products are available at special quantity discounts for bulk purchase for sales promotions, premiums, fundraising, and educational needs. For details, write Charisma House Book Group, 600 Rinehart Road, Lake Mary, Florida 32746, or telephone (407) 333-0600.

LIFE WITH THE HOLY SPIRIT by Katherine Ruonala
Published by Charisma House
Charisma Media/Charisma House Book Group
600 Rinehart Road
Lake Mary, Florida 32746
www.charismahouse.com

Unless otherwise noted, all Scripture quotations are taken from the Modern English Version. Copyright © 2014 by Military Bible Association. Used by permission. All rights reserved.

Scripture quotations marked AMP are from the Amplified Bible. Copyright © 2015 by The Lockman Foundation, La Habra, CA 90631. All rights reserved. Used by permission.

Scripture quotations marked KJV are from the King James Version of the Bible.

Scripture quotations marked NKJV are taken from the New King James Version®. Copyright © 1982 by Thomas Nelson. Used by permission. All rights reserved.

Scripture quotations marked NLT are from the Holy Bible, New Living Translation, copyright © 1996, 2004, 2007. Used by permission of Tyndale House Publishers, Inc., Wheaton, IL 60189. All rights reserved.

Scripture quotations marked THE MESSAGE are from *The Message: The Bible in Contemporary English*, copyright © 1993, 1994, 1995, 1996, 2000, 2001, 2002. Used by permission of NavPress Publishing Group.

Cover design by Justin Evans

Visit the author's website at KatherineRuonala.com.

Library of Congress Cataloging-in-Publication Data:
Names: Ruonala, Katherine, author.
Title: Life with the Holy Spirit / Katherine Ruonala.
Description: Lake Mary, Florida : Charisma House, 2017.
Identifiers: LCCN 2016059374| ISBN 9781629990828 (trade paper) | ISBN
    9781629990835 (ebook)
Subjects: LCSH: Holy Spirit.
Classification: LCC BT121.3 .R86 2017 | DDC 231/.3--dc23
LC record available at https://lccn.loc.gov/2016059374

All miraculous healings and supernatural experiences recounted in this book were either witnessed by the author or shared with her by the person or people involved.

Some names and identifying details have been changed to protect the privacy of individuals.

While the author has made every effort to provide accurate telephone numbers and Internet addresses at the time of publication, neither the publisher nor the author assumes any responsibility for errors or for changes that occur after publication.

18 19 20 21 22 — 10 9 8 7 6 5 4 3
Printed in the United States of America

I want to dedicate this book to all those who are hungering for a deeper relationship with the Holy Spirit. It is my prayer that this book would be a help and an encouragement to you as you learn to lean on the One who loves you more than you will ever know.

CONTENTS

ACKNOWLEDGMENTS

I WANT TO GIVE all thanks and honor to God for His kindness to us. Without the power and help of His Holy Spirit none of this would have been possible.

To my wonderful family—Tom, Jessica, Emily, and Joseph—thank you for your love, support, and encouragement. You mean more to me than I can express.

To Emily Harland, Sheila Williams, Chris Tiegreen, Sarah Cheesman, Mark Greenwood, Helen Cobanov, Kelly Horne, and my mother, Roslyn Mills, thank you for your help with the editing process. Your input has been so valuable.

To all those who intercede for me—particularly Jenny Haggar, Sharon Wilks, and Deborah Cook—thank you for your constant love, support, and intercession.

To our Glory City Churches and all my ministry partners, thank you for your love and support. I so appreciate your love for God and for us and your helping us take the good news of the gospel to the world.

FOREWORD

REVIVAL IS STIRRING, and the movement of the Holy Spirit is manifesting mightily across the nations.

Kathcrine is known around the world for having a powerful prophetic and healing ministry. What many don't realize is that behind the signs and wonders that follow Katherine is a lifelong, joyful dependence on the Holy Spirit, which has birthed her latest book, *Life With the Holy Spirit*.

Life With the Holy Spirit is a wake-up call to the church encouraging the sons and daughters of God to grab ahold of their true identities in Christ and respond to Jesus's invitation for us to operate in the fullness of the promises we have been given: "He who believes in Me will do the works that I do also. And he will do greater works than these, because I am going to My Father" (John 14:12). Katherine reminds us that now is a time of greater revelation and miracles, but the key always has been and always will be our partnership with the Holy Spirit.

In 2 Corinthians 13:14 the apostle Paul prays a blessing over the Corinthian church that "the grace of the Lord Jesus Christ, and the love of God, and the communion of the Holy Spirit be with [them] all." Katherine artfully communicates how the overflow of our connection and sense of the Holy Spirit's direction will naturally produce an increase in the signs and wonders that follow, as well as a personal revival in our creativity, prophecy, destiny, purpose, dreams, love, and ability to overcome. *Life With the Holy Spirit* inspires hope in seeing the impossible be made possible and ignites hunger for the most precious gift of all—intimate relationship with the Holy Spirit.

—Dr. Ché Ahn
President, Harvest International Ministry
Founding Pastor, HRock Church, Pasadena, California
International Chancellor, Wagner Leadership
Institute

INTRODUCTION

PEOPLE WERE COMING from all around for healing. Some flew in from the other side of the country and came to the meeting with their suitcases, and others had driven twelve hours to be there. They were desperate to be healed, and many received wonderful miracles. We saw God do some incredible things. As I looked at these people making such a huge effort to get to the meetings, my heart went out to them.

Later that week I was in Los Angeles at a pastors meeting, and during one of the meetings I felt compelled to contend with God in prayer about what I was feeling. "Lord, I want to see them *all* healed," my spirit cried out to Him. "This is not too much to ask. This is what happened when You were on earth. You even said we would do 'greater works' than the works You had been doing" (John 14:12). It is true that Jesus didn't heal every sick person on the planet, but Scripture tells us He did heal everyone who came to Him for help, and that was without exception. The more I thought about it, the more compassion I felt for people and the more fervently I was compelled to pray. Despite the experiences of many ministers throughout modern history, I knew this was not too big a request. After all, "it is no longer [we] who live, but Christ who lives in [us]" (Gal. 2:20). So as I sat in the meeting, I kept silently crying out, "Lord, I want everyone who looks to You for healing in my meetings to be healed. This is a totally reasonable request. You are the same yesterday, today, and forever; it is not too much to ask that You heal them all!"

As the other pastors and I walked to the car that night, a stranger walking with two large dogs came toward me. That's not what you expect to see late at night in a Los Angeles parking lot, but he came straight up to me and said, "Pick a number between one and twenty-two."

"Um…hi. I'm Katherine. What's your name?" I asked.

"My name's Michael. Pick a number between one and twenty-two."

So I chose a number. I can't even remember what it was.

He opened a Bible he had been carrying with him and said, "I've got a Scripture verse for you!" Then he read, "And He healed them all" (Matt. 12:15). He closed his Bible and walked off. He didn't talk to anyone else; he just left.

Either someone was sent on assignment from God, or I'd had an encounter with an angel. Either way, I knew the Lord was speaking.

I believe that God does not want us to settle for seeing a few people get healed. We get very excited about one miracle, and we should. As I am writing this, I have just come from a meeting in the United Kingdom where three people with totally deaf ears were healed one after the other. Six people with totally deaf ears have been healed in the past three weeks.

I love to hear these testimonies, but we must press in for more. God wants us to contend for our inheritance, which is to see greater works than Jesus did. We are created in His image, and He lives in us. We don't have just an echo or a shadow of Christ in us. He didn't give us just a little bit of Himself. Jesus told us His Spirit would live in us and be upon us as the Spirit was upon Him, and we would do "greater works" (John 14:12). We are destined to go "from glory to glory" (2 Cor. 3:18). "It is no longer [we] who live, but Christ who lives in [us]" (Gal. 2:20). God Himself is now working through us.

Somehow in our human thinking we try to interpret these wonderful promises as things we get to taste only a little bit of or get a small glimpse of, as if we get only a piece of who Jesus really is. We see ourselves as faint reflections of the true glory.

The heart of our Father longs for us to wake up. He wants the eyes of our understanding to be enlightened in the knowledge of Him because if we have an understanding of who He is, we will know the hope of our calling (Eph. 1:17–18). When we understand who He is, we can recognize who we are—our true identity is in Him. We get revelation about Him, which gives us revelation about ourselves. We recognize, "That's what I'm like." "As He is, so are we in this world" (1 John 4:17). As we behold Him, we are "transformed into the same image" (2 Cor. 3:18). We realize we are not weak, frail human beings. We begin to see that it really is "no longer [we] who live, but Christ who lives in [us]" (Gal. 2:20). We step out of the deception of thinking we're just a shadow and into the reality of our true selves in Him. The invitation into divine revelation and acceleration right now is extraordinary, and God is waiting for His people to respond to it. He is offering us the fullness of His promises.

We can't step into those promises without help. In fact, we can't step into them at all unless we learn how to partner with the Holy Spirit. It is His power that does the work, and without Him we can do nothing. As believers our lives now belong to Him, and He is the One who works within us. He is the manifestation of God through us. Anytime someone gets healed or delivered, or anytime there's supernatural revelation and insight, it's because the Holy Spirit is at work. For us to do the "greater works," we have to live in fellowship with Him and cooperate with what He is doing.

That's what this book is about—life with the Holy Spirit. God is doing amazing things in this season, and He is preparing His people for an even greater manifestation of who He is. The Holy Spirit is extending an invitation into a realm of glory few have ever experienced. He wants to reveal Himself to the world to such a degree that the knowledge of God's glory covers the earth "as the waters cover the seas" (Hab. 2:14). He wants us to experience unprecedented breakthrough. But it won't happen if we just run our ministries as usual and keep inviting Him to endorse our plans. We have to learn how to recognize what He is doing and cooperate with Him. We are being called to enter into a deep fellowship with the Trinity and respond to the Spirit's leading.

Many people struggle with understanding how to relate to God as one in three persons, as a triune being. I did for many years. There were times when I didn't even know if it was OK to talk to the Holy Spirit. I'll share that story in the pages to come, as I will many others about the process of getting to know Him, receiving His counsel and comfort, walking in His freedom, ministering in His power, resting in His strength, bearing His fruit, praying His prayers, dreaming His dreams, and fellowshipping with Him as a friend. For many people the Holy Spirit is the unknown member of the Trinity, but He invites us to know Him as our closest companion.

My relationship with the Holy Spirit has grown dramatically over the years as I've asked Him to take me by the hand and teach me. He has been faithful to show me how deeply He loves me, what He has been planning for me, and how I can partner with Him to see His purposes accomplished. And He will do the same for you. The Holy Spirit enjoys you. He wants to teach you about His ways and show you how to receive every one of His wonderful promises. He is looking forward to your companionship.

Chapter 1

GOD THE FATHER, SON, AND HOLY SPIRIT

I STILL REMEMBER ALL the cliques from the girls school I went to. There were the academic people who did math and physics; they always stuck together. Then there were sporty people, the athletes. And, of course, there was the clique of really popular people—that was an especially exclusive one. And then there was the group of people who were just kind enough to let anybody in who wasn't able to get into the other cliques. That's the one I was in. It's easy in that kind of culture to grow up with a sense of rejection. Cliques can cause an enormous amount of stress. They can make you feel lonely even when you're surrounded by people.

God is extremely relational, and He is not at all exclusive with people who will recognize who He is and come to Him in faith. In fact, He welcomes us with open arms into a relationship with Him. He delights in revealing Himself and sharing His nature with us. He wants to show off who He is. He is eternal, omniscient, omnipresent, and

1

omnipotent. He is love, light, spirit, truth, Creator, and more. He actually wants us to be in awe of that and appreciate His wonders and majesty. He is to be worshipped as one truly amazing, overwhelming, staggeringly beautiful being.

God is not relational only with us. He is relational within Himself. Although He is one God, He is also a family—a perfectly harmonious fellowship of one being in three persons. And astonishingly He invites us into that fellowship to enjoy it and celebrate it forever.

Three Persons in One God

We've seen many people come to the Lord recently from all sorts of backgrounds. One of the questions that come up often among those who have come to Christ, especially from a monotheistic background such as Judaism or Islam, is about the Trinity. How can there be one God yet three persons—the Father, the Son, and the Holy Spirit? How can Christians believe in one God and three Gods all at once? Of course, we don't believe in three Gods—He is one. But we do know Him as God in three persons.

We see the Holy Spirit introduced in the earliest pages of Scripture. In the very beginning, in Genesis, we read, "God created the heavens and the earth. The earth was formless and void, darkness was over the surface of the deep, and the Spirit of God was moving over the surface of the water" (Gen. 1:1–2). So the Holy Spirit is introduced right at the beginning. He isn't a New Testament phenomenon. He has always existed because He is God, along with the Father and the Son. God says a few verses later,

"Let us make man in our image, after our likeness....So God created man in His own image; in the image of God He created him; male and female He created them" (vv. 26–27). Even in the beginning, the one God is plural: "us." That is hard for finite minds to grasp, but it's true. He is three persons just as we, created in His image, are tripartite beings made up of body, soul, and spirit.

All three persons of God are mentioned in Scripture in the story of Jesus's baptism:

> When all the people were baptized, and when Jesus also had been baptized and was praying, the heavens were opened, and the Holy Spirit descended in a bodily form like a dove on Him, and a voice came from heaven which said, "You are My beloved Son. In You I am well pleased."
>
> —Luke 3:21–22

This is a remarkable picture of the Trinity: the Son communing with the Father in prayer; the Holy Spirit coming upon Him in "bodily form like a dove," anointing Him; and the Father testifying that Jesus is His Son. Within the Trinity, there is absolute love, honor, and delight. They love one another perfectly. And we are invited into this perfect love.

We don't need to be able to explain the Trinity in order to accept what Scripture says about it, but there are some illustrations that capture the idea of three entities in one. I've heard it said that the Trinity is similar to trying to explain time. The past, present, and future are all distinct things, but they are all time. Ice, water, and steam have distinct properties, but they are all H_2O—one essence in three different forms. In the same way, God is Father, Son, and Spirit, but all are God. Scripture doesn't explain this fully—obviously God is a lot more complex and a lot more personal than time and water—but it clearly does point to the Trinity. Jesus told His followers to go and baptize in the name of the Father, Son, and Spirit (Matt. 28:19). Both the Father and the Son are referred to as the first and the last, the Alpha and the Omega (Isa. 44:6; 48:12; Rev. 1:8, 11; 22:13). Romans 8:9–11 and other passages use "the Spirit of God" and "the Spirit of Christ" interchangeably. These are just a few examples among many of biblical references to the three persons of the Trinity. God included them in His Word because He wants us to understand who He is and to experience Him in every way.

The Holy Spirit is with us on earth, empowering us to connect in a very real and relational way to the Father and Son, and He is often described in the Bible as the Spirit of the Father and the Spirit of Christ (Matt. 10:20; Gal. 4:6). So in order to appreciate who the Holy Spirit is and why we need to develop deep, personal relationship with Him, we first need to understand who God the Father and God the Son are.

God the Father

I find it easy to relate to God as Father. We often begin our prayers with "Our Father," just as Jesus taught (Matt. 6:9). In fact, the Holy Spirit empowers us to cry out, "Abba, Father" (Rom. 8:15; Gal. 4:6)—a phrase that means "Papa" or "Daddy."[1] The Spirit is crying out within us, helping us to understand that we are connected with the Godhead. We are in the family! The Spirit of the Son lives in us as children who have been adopted by the Father.

My parents divorced when I was four, and I didn't get to see much of my father when I was growing up. He lived about twelve hours away in New South Wales, Australia, and I got to see him only a few weeks twice a year. I loved being with him and found it hard to leave. I remember very early one morning when I was about ten he woke us before dawn so we could catch a light aircraft to begin our journey back to Brisbane, Queensland, Australia. He was stern when I protested leaving, but when I was on the plane, I remember looking out the window and seeing him wipe away tears. Even today I sense a little touch of sadness in his voice when it is time to say good-bye. This reminds me of how much our heavenly Father loves us. The Bible tells us His thoughts toward us are more than we can number.

My father is a wonderful man—an intelligent doctor who loves poetry and a good philosophical debate. I absolutely adore him. But because I didn't see him very much as a child, my heart really yearned for a father's love. I needed the heavenly Father to fill the desperate need in my heart for a father. We all need this; even fathers who are with their children all the time cannot meet the need a child has for the perfect father. No man on earth can fill that role. God is the Father who doesn't sleep. He is always there, always safe, always wise, always reliable, and always faithful. He never lets us down, never disappoints, and never fails.

I often find myself crying out, "Abba," when I'm speaking my heavenly language. That is the Spirit of God helping me recognize that I am accepted in the family of God. He wants His children to embrace the lavish love and affection of their Father. We can run into His presence without being afraid. We can come boldly to the "throne of grace" (Heb. 4:16). He has made a way for us to be intimately connected. As believers we are no longer separated from the Father by sin because in Jesus we have been given the faith and grace to exchange our sin for His righteousness. No shame should ever keep us at a distance because He has done away with our shame. No problem or obstacle can stand in the way of our connection with Him. Nothing in all of creation can "separate us from the love of [our Father]" (Rom. 8:38–39). He invites us to come running into His presence and call Him "Papa" without any reservation at all.

Abba is actually the most intimate term you can use with a father, and the fact that the Spirit inspires this cry in us shows us what kind of relationship God wants us to have with Him. Many people view God as an authoritarian, with Jesus pleading with Him not to be angry with us. But that's not the picture the Bible gives us; that's not who our Father is. Because He has made a way for us to come to Him, He opens His arms to welcome us. When something goes wrong, He is on our side and longing to help. He is always available, and He always knows what to do. We can go to Him and talk to Him anytime, and He never gets tired of it. He is there for us, and He is worthy of our absolute respect, adoration, and worship. God is everything we could possibly want in a father.

If you're one of the many people who feel they've been let down by a father, this is wonderful news, isn't it? It's wonderful news even for those who have had loving, available fathers. I feel so spoiled because I have this perfect Father who adores me. I'm Daddy's little girl, His special daughter—His favorite! My heart's desire and my prayer is that you would know that you're His favorite too, that you would know how accepted and adored you are by your Father.

God the Son

The Holy Spirit is the "Spirit of Jesus" (Phil. 1:19). God the Son came to us in the form of flesh, walked the earth with us, and didn't sin. Because He didn't sin, He could be the perfect sacrifice, "the Lamb of God, who takes away the sin of the world" (John 1:29). Sin separates us from God, and without the Son's coming and laying down His life for us, being crucified in our place—Scripture says in 2 Corinthians 5:21 that He even became sin for us—we could not be connected to the Father. We would have to remain outside the family of God and be forever separated from Him. God loved us too much for that. He sent Jesus to make a way to bring us into intimate union with Him.

The blood of Jesus accomplished that by taking away our sin. His blood offers forgiveness of sin and restores us to a place of connectedness, blessing, and favor. The Bible says Jesus "was wounded for our transgressions, he was bruised for our iniquities," that "the chastisement of our peace was upon him, and by his stripes we are healed" (Isa. 53:5). By the power of His blood, we receive not only forgiveness but also restoration and healing!

A lot is included in that promise. The fact that Jesus was "wounded for our transgressions" means that He took the punishment for our sins so we would not have to be punished. We don't have to beat ourselves up. To receive eternal salvation you only have to believe and confess that Jesus is the Son of God and therefore is qualified to save you. In faith you need to exchange your sin for His righteousness. Repent and say: "Jesus, have mercy on me. Forgive me for my sin. I need forgiveness, and I believe You are faithful and just to forgive me. I believe that the blood of Jesus releases me from the penalty of sin and that You give me the power to be different. I receive Your forgiveness and cleansing." By faith we must then deliberately cast down any thought that is contrary to the truth that we are made clean by His blood. We must live by faith in what the Son's sacrifice has accomplished.

Jesus made the way for us to actually become brand-new creations (2 Cor. 5:17). All who are born again out of the death and resurrection of Jesus have been restored to the image and nature of God. Now we live with a new identity. We have been made holy. When you sin, the Holy Spirit wants to help you repent, recognize that what you have done is wrong, and receive by faith the forgiveness that comes through Jesus. The Holy Spirit within you wants to help you remember and live fully aware of your new identity. As believers we are no longer defined by our sin but by the nature of Christ.

Jesus is our compass. Paul wrote that he "determined not to know anything among [the Corinthians] except Jesus Christ and Him crucified" (1 Cor. 2:2). He is to be the center of our preaching, our thoughts, our worship, our relationship with the Father—everything. I've seen plenty of people become fascinated with extra-biblical things and spiritual power. But we must determine to be fascinated with nothing but Christ and the fact that He has made the way for us to have fellowship with God. We have to determine to know nothing but Jesus because He is our Savior, the Way, the Truth, the Life, the hope of glory, the mediator of the new covenant, and the exact image of the Father Himself. We could talk about Him forever. We worship Him, lift Him up, and give Him glory because He is the One who suffered, died, rose again, and is seated at the right hand of the Father, and we are seated with Him as fellow heirs of His kingdom. Every promise that relates to Him is ours too.

If you've ever felt as if you're on the outside, you can put that behind you now. God has given His life so we can be part of the best in-crowd there is. He welcomes us into fellowship with the Trinity, the family of God. That beats any of those cliques of popular, intelligent, or athletic people I used to see at school. I think Jesus must have been smiling when His disciples were discussing who would get to sit on His right and His left in the kingdom (Mark 10:37). Ephesians tells us that as believers we are now seated in heavenly places with Him, and He's seated at the Father's right hand (Eph. 1:20; 2:6). That's where I'm seated now! Jesus is in the most favored place in heaven, and we're seated right there with Him. It really doesn't get any better than that.

God the Holy Spirit

When we are first introduced to the Holy Spirit in Scripture, He is hovering over the face of the waters. Later we read about His manifesting in the physical form of a dove. Then we see Him as a "mighty rushing wind" and "tongues...of fire" (Acts 2:2–3). Jesus speaks of Him as the One who will be not only with us but also within us to help, counsel, comfort, empower, lead, and teach us—God in a personal and present form. So who is He? A force? A dove? Wind? Fire? Or is He a knowable person?

The Holy Spirit is the third person of the Trinity and will relate to us and reveal Himself to us in many ways to help us know Him. He has come to dwell in us, His temple (1 Cor. 6:19), and to clothe us with His power. The Holy Spirit has revealed Himself to me as God in person literally standing in the room with me, sitting with me on my piano stool, and sitting in the car beside me as I am driving. I have experienced His power moving within me and coming upon me in ways that have left me in holy fear, speechless, and in awe, sometimes unable even to move. And the Holy Spirit wants to reveal Himself to you every day in wonderful ways.

The night before His crucifixion Jesus told His disciples the wonderful news that God the Holy Spirit was going to come and stay with them for the rest of their lives. "It is to your *advantage* that I go away; for if I do not go away, the Helper will not come to you; but if I depart, I will send

Him to you" (John 16:7, NKJV, emphasis added). The disciples had to have been incredulous. How could it possibly be better for them if Jesus went away? But the Holy Spirit is not some faint whiff of God's essence; He isn't just an echo of the divine presence. He is God.

When we begin to understand what it means to have fellowship with the Spirit of God and know who He is and how He works, we will wake up to the revelation that we carry His supernatural power. God does not want us to sit around, simply longing for the day we get to go home and be with Him. It's true that we have a lot to look forward to, but He has also given us much to experience now. He wants us to recognize that He is with us in the here and now and that we can be just like Him. "As He is, so are we in this world" (1 John 4:17). We are ambassadors of Christ, not only looking forward to our heavenly home but also enjoying the fact that He is with us in the moment. When we die, we will be with Him forever in eternity. But we already are with Him. As Jesus said, it is better having the Holy Spirit with us than having Him still here, walking the earth in physical form. Now God is not just *with* us; He is *in* us (1 Cor. 6:19). That's not a promissory note. It's for now.

I used to get confused about the concept of the Holy Spirit, especially as I heard people talk to the Father and the Son but never the Spirit. I didn't even know if we were allowed to talk to Him. I'd heard that the Spirit always points us toward Jesus and toward the Father, which meant to me that He wanted to divert attention away from Himself. And it's true that He points to Jesus and the

Father; it's the Spirit who draws people to Jesus and cries out, "Abba," within us. He constantly reminds us that our Father is good and loves us very much. He reminds us of the words of Jesus, just as Jesus promised He would. But it works the other way too. The Father and the Son talk about the Spirit all the time. This isn't a hierarchy; the three are equal in their oneness. The Holy Spirit is with us on earth to help us know the Trinity—fellowshipping with us Himself while continually testifying to us of the Father and Son in heaven and helping us understand the family and the kingdom to which we now belong.

We don't have to tiptoe around the Holy Spirit. He is actually very much on our side. He is our Advocate, our Comforter, our helper, our teacher, and our guide. He's the One with whom we can have genuine, intimate fellowship. He wants us to know what it means to be close to Him, and He enjoys fellowship with us.

I went to an Anglican girls school when I was young, and we would say a benediction at every assembly: "May the grace of our Lord Jesus Christ, the love of God, and the fellowship of the Holy Spirit be with us all this day and forevermore. Amen." We would say it fast, without a breath from beginning to end, and then get on with our day. This benediction actually comes from Scripture—2 Corinthians 13:14. Later on in life when I was listening to an audio Bible in the car that verse came up, and I heard it with new ears. The word *fellowship* suddenly hit me. The grace of the Lord Jesus—which gives us access to God, includes us in the family of God, immerses us in His love, and makes us the apple of His eye—is all about fellowship. Because of the grace of Jesus, we can now have intimate relationship with His Spirit. I said, "God, I really want to understand this. I want to know how to interact with You in a way that isn't irreverent or wrong but is true fellowship." And what I found is that it's just hanging out with Him, having conversation, and doing life together. It isn't technical or formal. It isn't a cold doctrine. It's actually fun. It was very exciting to me that God said He wanted to have fellowship with me.

His fellowship is precious to me. I need friendship that goes beyond the capacity of people to fulfill. No one is able to be available to me 24/7, but the Holy Spirit is always there for me and never lets me down or gets frustrated with me. He fills all my deepest needs. The Holy Spirit loves it when I acknowledge His presence and companionship. He listens to and understands my every thought. He is ready to hear every emotion I have, every problem I want to talk about, every issue I want to process with Him. He doesn't mind that I'm a verbal processor. I don't have to worry about talking His ear off. He's happy to listen because He enjoys my company. The Holy Spirit is more attentive and caring than any spouse, friend, or parent ever could be, and the very thought of His consistently kind and unselfish love overwhelms me.

Deep down everyone would love a companion like this. Every one of us desires this kind of friendship with the Spirit because that's what we were made for. We were created for love. When you were born again a desire for genuine fellowship with the Spirit was born in you at the same time. Your spirit wants to talk with God's Spirit.

My question about whether it was permissible to talk to the Spirit was something I had to process. I thought, "If He's my Comforter and Counselor and teacher, as Jesus said He is, then I must be able to talk to Him. How can you learn anything from a teacher or receive counsel from him if you can't have a conversation with him?" So with trepidation I tried it out one day. I began to ask the Holy Spirit for help.

The first day I tried this I was driving to a meeting. "Holy Spirit," I began—feeling as if I should apologize for talking to Him but going on anyway—"Holy Spirit, I believe I'm allowed to talk to You because You're my teacher, so I've got a few questions. Would You teach me about the falling down thing?" At the time I wasn't sure why people fell down in meetings when someone laid hands on them or prayed for them, and I wondered if they were pushed, if they just did a courtesy drop, or if they really did fall under God's power. "I'd really like to know about that. And also can You please heal me of the ganglion cyst on my wrist? And will You take away the fear that my husband might die?"

That's quite a range of questions, but that was what had been going through my mind. The cyst was something that had been there for a while, and I was very ready for it to go. The fear that my husband would die was something I had really been wrestling with. I was twenty-three at the time and had been married for three years, and I was so glad I had found someone to love me. Tom had signed a piece of paper and made vows saying he would love me till he died, so, insecure as I was, I thought, "What if he dies?

Who will love me then?" I was tormented by this nagging question because I didn't yet understand that God wanted to be the One who filled my need for love. I needed to be free from that fear, so I simply asked the Spirit for what was on my heart.

At the meeting the preacher called for anyone who had fasted and prayed for healing to come up. I didn't think I qualified because I had been eating cakes all day, but I had skipped dinner, and I'd also read some scripture, which happened to be the passage he had preached on. So I thought maybe it would be all right. I was at the end of the line, and long before he got to me I found myself flat on the floor. When he finally got to me, he asked the ushers to pick me up and said, "Oppression, go!" I immediately hit the floor again. No one had touched me; I was just overwhelmed by the power of God. I knew the Holy Spirit had just answered my first question. While I was on the floor, the Spirit set me free from fear. I was trembling, and I saw the face of Jesus. He said, "Katherine, I'm setting you free from everything." And I was different from that day forward. I noticed a few days later that the cyst on my wrist was gone.

I began to understand that the Holy Spirit loves it when we talk to Him. There was nothing to be afraid of, and what He did for me was better than I could have imagined. So after that I began having conversations with Him all the time. I'd sit at the piano playing, and I'd be aware that He was with me—in me, as He promised, but also just hanging out with me, as if He were sitting right there on the piano stool with me. I began to acknowledge the person of the Holy Spirit with me and in me, just as the Bible says: "Lean not on your own understanding; in all your ways acknowledge Him" (Prov. 3:5–6). And things began to get glorious. I became aware of His presence. I started having visions relating to God's heart for the lost. I began to prophesy and intercede as never before. A deep hunger for God was stirred within me. A desperation for a baptism of fire stirred in me, and I began to seek God with a fervor I had never known before. Within months I was having encounters with God that I can describe only as a baptism of fire that changed me forever. I went to a movie with a friend and, aware that the Holy Spirit was there with me, I found that I couldn't stay. I had to get up and leave because I was aware that the Spirit didn't like it. My daily life began to change as I realized how connected we were. I realized I didn't ever have to do anything on my own. And I began to share His love for people and His desire to demonstrate that love through miracles, signs, and wonders.

The cry of my heart that I shared in the introduction—that all would be healed—stems from fellowship with the Holy Spirit because this is His heart! It isn't too much to ask, not if He is the One working through us as we lean into His strength and let His power flow. I believe the Holy Spirit is longing to teach us what it means to have a relationship with Him, to have fellowship with Him all the time, to be aware of His presence when we lie down and when we get up. Consciously thinking about the person of the Holy Spirit's being with us heightens our sensitivity to Him. Because of what Jesus has done, we are no longer just individuals. That may offend those who take pride in their individuality, but if you're born again, being an individual is not God's highest will for you. You are unique, of course, but you are not created to walk separately from or independently of God. God's will is for each of us to be joined into His family and to be one with Him. Jesus's prayer was that His followers would be one—with one another and with Him—just as He and the Father are one (John 17:21). When we understand that and enter into the fellowship of the Holy Spirit, everything we do is with Him and in Him. It's an opportunity for us to activate faith. We get to be Christlike, as Christ is living in us. We live life in the power of the Spirit. And we begin to do the works of the Father, just as Jesus promised.

Chapter 2

THE FELLOWSHIP OF
THE HOLY SPIRIT

I WAS WORSHIPPING THE Lord one night not long ago and having a beautiful time with Him when I saw a vision. I saw myself sitting in a window frame on a summer's day. There were some things in my heart I was anxious about, and as I was looking out the window, the Holy Spirit came and sat down right beside me. He reminded me of some scriptures and gave me some promises. There was nothing stern about it; He brought me great peace and put me completely at ease. That's what He does. His presence changes everything.

That vision was a precious reminder to me of the kind of fellowship the Holy Spirit wants to have with us. He wants us to live in that fellowship and have a continual awareness of His presence so we can live in perfect peace. Peace is one of the fruit of the Spirit, one of the by-products of being with Him. Simply by spending time with Him we become peaceful because He calms all our fears. He is perfect love and fullness of joy. All the beautiful fruit

19

of the Spirit becomes part of our character, not from going after the fruit but as a result of knowing Him and of His living in us. As we spend time getting to know Him, we become like Him.

If that's true, then it's important for us to know a bit about what the Spirit is like. Who is He, really? If we are invited into this wonderful family of God—to have fellowship with the Father, Son, and Spirit—what should we expect the culture of that beautiful family to be like? Because the Spirit is God along with the Father and the Son, they all share the same character traits. Their roles may be different, but their characters are the same. God is loving, patient, kind, wise, and powerful, and always will be. Since we are in active partnership with the Holy Spirit, we need to know how He ministers to us and through us.

The Roles of the Holy Spirit

No discussion of any person of the Trinity can be comprehensive. We are, after all, talking about an infinite God. But Scripture does make some clear statements about who the Holy Spirit is and what He does.

The Holy Spirit is our teacher.

Teaching and learning involve much more than the impartation of information. A true teacher is available to mentor, train, discuss, correct, answer questions, and walk with a learner through difficult situations. The Holy Spirit is a true teacher, always present and always willing to guide us. That means we can talk to Him and ask Him questions and expect Him to answer. He is the most comprehensive, prophetic, powerful teacher we could ever ask for (John 14:26; 1 Cor. 2:13). As the Spirit of truth the Holy Spirit wants to guide us into all truth, and as our prophetic teacher He will tell us things to come (John 16:13). Not only does He want to give us information, but He also wants to help us experience and apply that knowledge in practical and life-changing ways (Eph. 3:19). He trains us in a kingdom lifestyle.

The Holy Spirit reveals truth.

As you will see in the coming pages, my mind can very often follow trains of thought that are not exactly true. You have probably already discovered that yours can too. So I am extremely grateful that one of the Holy Spirit's roles is to guide us into all truth (John 16:13). Not only did He do this by inspiring the words of Scripture and applying them to our lives (2 Tim. 3:16), but He also continues to do it through a number of ways as we relate to Him. He reveals to us the wisdom and insights of the Father (Eph. 1:17; 1 Cor. 2:10–12) so we can have the mind of Christ (1 Cor. 2:16). He always brings us back to the heart of the Father.

The Holy Spirit is our Comforter.

One of the most precious gifts I have been given is to know the Holy Spirit as my Comforter (John 14:26, KJV; Acts 9:31). There have been days I have walked and talked with Him and felt His arm around me as I have cried. He interprets my tears, listening to me as I pour out my heart to Him. The Passion Translation of Psalm 38:9 says, "Lord, you know all my desires and deepest longings. My tears are liquid words and you can read them all." He is my most trusted and faithful friend. The Holy Spirit has spoken words of comfort to my heart as I have fellowshipped with Him in the daytime, and He has comforted me with revelation through my dreams at night. We will go much deeper into the Holy Spirit's role as a comforter in the following chapters and discover how comprehensively He meets the needs of our hearts.

The Holy Spirit is the Spirit of wisdom.

The Holy Spirit is also "the spirit of wisdom and revelation" (Eph. 1:17). I am very aware of my constant need for the wisdom of God. As I have been reading the Book of Proverbs recently, I have felt a greater desire to be deliberate in taking time to fellowship with the Spirit of wisdom. Proverbs describes wisdom as a person, and I believe that person is the Holy Spirit. By seeking to spend time fellowshipping with the Holy Spirit intentionally as the Spirit of wisdom, I have been surprised at the thoughts and ideas I have had. James 1:5 says, "If any of you lacks wisdom, let him ask of God, who gives to all men liberally and without criticism, and it will be given to him." The Holy Spirit loves it when you seek Him for wisdom, and He wants to surprise you with His wonderful ideas in your everyday life.

The Holy Spirit empowers us to manifest His fruit and His gifts.

Because "it is no longer [we] who live, but Christ who lives in [us]" (Gal. 2:20), we have the power to bear the fruit of Christ's Spirit. We don't need to try to manifest

His fruit. We simply come into agreement with the truth of our new identity, and His fruit will become evident in us. Abiding in Jesus we will bear much fruit, for we can do nothing without Him (John 15:5). As the Holy Spirit helps us remember that "it is no longer [we] who live, but [Christ's Spirit] who lives in [us]," we can have faith to produce the fruit of His Spirit in our everyday lives.

An apple tree can't produce peaches because its identity as an apple tree dictates what it produces. In the same way our understanding of our identity dictates our fruit. As people rooted and grounded in Jesus, the tree of life, we can have faith so that it is normal for us to produce the fruit of Jesus's Spirit—"love, joy, peace, [longsuffering], gentleness, goodness, faith, meekness, and self-control" (Gal. 5:22–23). As believers we are not operating out of the tree of the knowledge of good and evil, trying to avoid evil and be good. We have been set free from the law and grafted into the tree of life, Jesus, and through His Spirit in us we can produce good fruit as we remember who we are.

Just as we are empowered to bear the fruit of the Holy Spirit, we also are empowered to manifest His gifts (1 Cor. 12:4–11). Every believer has one or more gifts that demonstrate who God is, impart His will and His truth into the lives of His people, and unite us in interdependence with one another. In fact, we cannot experience God as fully as He wants us to without experiencing the gifts of others, and they cannot experience Him as fully as He desires without benefiting from each of our gifts. The Spirit empowers the entire body of Christ to work together as one (1 Cor. 12:12–14; Rom. 12:4–5).

The Holy Spirit demonstrates God's power through us.

As those who are empowered by the Spirit to bear fruit and manifest gifts, we also demonstrate the acts of God Himself (1 Cor. 2:4). This is evident throughout the Book of Acts, as miracle after miracle gives testimony to the power and name of Jesus (Acts 1:8). It has also been evident at times throughout church history, and today we are seeing a virtual explosion of miraculous power as people are being healed and delivered and lives are being changed.

The Holy Spirit is a joy giver.

One of the desires of the Holy Spirit is to help us continually experience the same level of joy and acceptance that is flourishing within the Godhead. He wants us to feel welcome in that place of total acceptance. When you're feeling down, He's the Comforter. He reminds you how deeply loved and connected you are. He wants you to feel at home in your new family. It is through the power of the Holy Spirit that we experience "the joy of the LORD," which is our strength (Neh. 8:10) and is inexpressible and "full of glory" (1 Pet. 1:8). It is the joy of the Holy Spirit that empowers me in every area of my life. His joy is beyond a natural happiness; it is supernatural and available at all times regardless of circumstances. Often when I am about to pray for someone for healing, I start giggling with a delight that is supernatural because I am more aware of the Father's heart and desire to touch that person than I am of the presenting circumstance. People often comment on how joyful I am, and I know it is the Holy Spirit in me and upon me who is responsible for that. You are no longer on the outside looking in; you're one of the special ones. You belong.

There are many other roles of the Spirit.

These are only a few of the roles of the Holy Spirit, and of course they manifest in a variety of ways. As believers being conformed into the image of Jesus we can be baptized in the Spirit (Acts 1:5), anointed with the Spirit (Acts 10:38), set free by the Spirit (2 Cor. 3:17), empowered to pray by the Spirit (Rom. 8:26–27), convicted of truth and righteousness (John 16:8), empowered to speak by the Spirit (Mark 13:11), and so much more.

In partnering with the Spirit it is most important to remember that He is not operating outside of us but as one who has come to dwell within us (John 14:17). Scripture also expresses this as Christ living within us (Gal. 2:20; Col. 1:27). We are the temples in which He dwells (1 Cor. 3:16; 6:19). He has not come to visit; He has come to inhabit. He is our constant friend.

The Nature of the Holy Spirit

Just as important as knowing what the Holy Spirit does is knowing how He does it. What is He like? What kind of personality does He have? What is His nature? What will His voice sound like when we hear Him? We have seen that every member of the Trinity is loving, patient, kind, wise, powerful, gentle, generous, and more, yet many people still see the Holy Spirit through the lenses of their own wounds and misconceptions. In order to partner with Him—to recognize Him and grow to be like Him in His work—we need to know something of His personality. In addition to the previously mentioned characteristics of the Father, Son, and Spirit, a few more about the Spirit are worth mentioning.

The Holy Spirit is creative.

"The Spirit of God was moving over the surface of the water" (Gen. 1:2), and the Lord began to speak light and life into the darkness of the world. The Spirit was ready to do something; His creativity was about to take what was formless and turn it into something beautiful and good. We sometimes feel that creativity in worship, don't we? The Spirit is just hovering, ready to surprise us or take us in a different direction. That's why we have to learn to be flexible in our worship, so we don't just say, "Well, this is the way I like it." If we lean on the Spirit, we will discover He's creative and wants to do things in different ways at different times. If we say yes to His creative impulses and sense what He is saying to us, we can experience what He wants to manifest. We can even partner with Him to express His creativity. Divine creativity comes from heaven through our hearts and minds to do things in new and different ways.

Psalm 104:30 says, "When You send forth Your Spirit, they are created, and You renew the surface of the ground." Job 33:4 says, "The Spirit of God has made me, and the breath of the Almighty has given me life." He is the Creator who made each of us. When God breathed into Adam, He was breathing His Spirit (Gen. 2:7). There's a wonderful wordplay in Scripture among breath, wind, and Spirit—in both Hebrew and Greek, one word has all three meanings.[1] So God didn't just breathe into Adam; He "spirited" him (similar to how our word *inspire* literally means "to breathe into"[2]).And Jesus did the same when He breathed on His disciples and told them to receive the Spirit (John 20:22). His Spirit, His breath, gives life. God wants us to understand that as we fellowship with Him, we experience life in a very tangible way. "It is the Spirit who gives life. The flesh profits nothing" (John 6:63). The Spirit is the author of prophecy, which almost always has a very creative element to it. "No prophecy at any time was produced by the will of man, but holy men moved by the Holy Spirit spoke from God" (2 Pet. 1:21). When we are moved by the Spirit, we prophesy the creative words of the Spirit.

The Holy Spirit's creative power at work within us helps us in our everyday lives and work, and if we will learn to ask for His help in this area, He will empower us with creative solutions and ideas. He is the Spirit of wisdom and the source from which truly inspired art, poetry, and music flow, and He holds the key to creative, breakthrough technologies and ideas. By partnering with the Holy Spirit, we have access to the mind of God and the power to change the world.

The Spirit is omnipresent.

Just as our triune God is omniscient (all-knowing) and omnipotent (all-powerful), He is also omnipresent—everywhere at once. That's wonderful news because it means we don't have to compete for His attention. He

27

is with me 24/7 just as He is with you 24/7. This truth is expressed beautifully in Psalm 139:

> Where shall I go from Your spirit, or where shall I flee from Your presence? If I ascend to heaven, You are there; if I make my bed in Sheol, You are there. If I take the wings of the morning and dwell at the end of the sea, even there Your hand shall guide me, and Your right hand shall take hold of me.
> —PSALM 139:7–10

In other words, no matter what you do and no matter how far you run, the Holy Spirit is there. My father often quotes a poem called "The Hound of Heaven" by Francis Thompson, which describes how the Holy Spirit pursues us.[3]

> I fled Him, down the nights and down the days;
>   I fled Him, down the arches of the years;
> I fled Him, down the labyrinthine ways
>   Of my own mind; and in the mist of tears
> I hid from Him, and under running laughter.
>   Up vistaed hopes I sped;
>   And shot, precipitated,
> Adown Titanic glooms of chasmèd fears,
>   From those strong Feet that followed, followed
>   after.
>   But with unhurrying chase,
>   And unperturbèd pace,
>   Deliberate speed, majestic instancy,
>   They beat—and a Voice beat
>   More instant than the Feet—
> 'All things betray thee, who betrayest Me.' ...

As long as there is breath in your body—as long as there is hope—the Spirit will come after you to bring you into God's kingdom. He relentlessly tries to connect with you and bring you into the fellowship of His family.

> If I say, "Surely the darkness shall cover me,
>   and the light shall be as night about me,"
> even the darkness is not dark to You,
>   but the night shines as the day,
>   for the darkness is like light to You.
>
> You brought my inner parts into being;
>   You wove me in my mother's womb.
> I will praise you, for You made me with fear and
>   wonder;
>   marvelous are Your works,
>   and You know me completely.
> My frame was not hidden from You
>   when I was made in secret,
> and intricately put together in the lowest parts of
>   the earth.
>   Your eyes saw me unformed,
> yet in Your book
>   all my days were written,
>   before any of them came into being.
> How precious also are Your thoughts to me, O
>   God!
>   How great is the sum of them!
> If I should count them,
>   they are more in number than the sand;
> when I awake,
>   I am still with You.
>   —PSALM 139:11–18

I think that's the most beautiful poetry. You can just sense the desire of God's heart in it. The Holy Spirit is with you all the time—He was with you when you were in the womb, He is with you when you're asleep, and He is with you when you wake up. He's waiting for you. When you begin to acknowledge Him, He will say, "Yes! I love you! I've been here all along!" God is "a very present help in trouble" (Ps. 46:1, NKJV)—our ever-present rescuer in time of need. I don't know about you, but my time of need is all the time. If I didn't recognize that, I would miss out on the help He wants to give.

The Holy Spirit is jealous.

Like the Father, the Spirit wants a unique connection with us. He wants our hearts. He is jealous about being the One we turn to in our times of need. The idea of God's being jealous for me used to make me feel quite a bit of pressure. A lot of people interpret that as if we can't enjoy anything in life without making Him jealous. But that's not at all what Scripture means by His jealousy. It's true that we are to love Him above all else, but this is really more about His wanting to be our closest companion, helper, problem solver, and Comforter. Many of us try to comfort ourselves with TV or shopping or something else, while He's standing there jealously thinking, "I could help you with that! I know the way of escape for you out of this pain and fear. Talk to me!" He can do much better leading us through our problems than anything or anyone else can, and He really wants us to turn to Him for that.

When we acknowledge Him, we can begin to enjoy the gift that He is to us.

Many non-believers don't understand this. They see our dependency on God as a weakness. And it is, but it's a weakness that draws us into a place of strength—the fellowship of the family. We were created for this kind of fellowship. In fact, we were the only part of creation made in the image of God, and the reason we were is that God wanted a relationship with us. The first humans were walking and talking with God as insiders in the family. They experienced that sweet spot of unbroken fellowship, where they knew they were the apple of His eye.

Sin disrupted the fellowship, and after man fell, humanity no longer had a beautiful union with God. So Jesus came to rescue us. I think the hardest part of the rescue for this three-in-one union was what it would require of Jesus. In the Garden of Gethsemane the night before His crucifixion Jesus asked, "O My Father, if it is possible, let this cup pass from Me. Nevertheless, not as I will, but as You will" (Matt. 26:39). I believe Jesus was less concerned about the physical beatings and the pain of crucifixion, as horrible as those things would be, than He was overwhelmed by the idea of becoming sin on our behalf. "God made Him who knew no sin to be sin for us, that we might become the righteousness of God in Him" (2 Cor. 5:21). That would require Him to be rejected by and separated from both the Father and the Spirit. Their relationship would be broken as Jesus would take the consequences of our sin on Himself. The only way He could do that was by knowing and anticipating the joy set before

Him (Heb. 12:2). He was willing to have the Father turn His face away from Him in order to bring us into fellowship so we could experience the perfect love and intimacy of the Holy Spirit, the Son, and the Father for eternity.

The Holy Spirit Makes God's Love Real to Us

The Holy Spirit wants to help us experience the same love and intimacy the Father, Son, and Spirit have for one another. The perfect, glorious love they have for one another they also have for us! While we are still on earth, unable to physically see the faces of the Father and the Son adoring us, the Holy Spirit walks with us to supernaturally reveal them to us. Ephesians 4:30 says we were sealed in Him "for the day of redemption." It is through the revelation and power of the Holy Spirit that we as believers are able to relate to the Father and the Son. The Holy Spirit is here walking with us to show us what it is to have that wonderful fellowship by faith. His desire is for us to be able to experience divine connection in ever-increasing ways so we can always know how deeply loved by God we are. He helps us in our spirit to see His face looking at us and smiling at us with absolute adoration.

That's why Paul prays for us to have "the Spirit of wisdom and revelation in the knowledge of Him, [enlightening] the eyes of [our] understanding" of who He is (Eph. 1:17–18). The Spirit wants us to recognize the Father and the Son and to know we are part of their fellowship. We don't have to wait until we die to experience that connection. We can enjoy it now. In fact, we are already seated with

Jesus at the right hand of the Father (Eph. 2:6). Everyone who is born again has already been given the most favored place in heaven.

Jesus prayed a really remarkable prayer in John 17. We looked at it briefly earlier, but it's worth another look in greater detail because the implications of it are just astounding:

> I do not pray for these alone, but also for those who will believe in Me through their word, that they may all be one, as You, Father, are in Me, and I in You. May they also be one in Us, that the world may believe that You have sent Me. I have given them the glory which You gave Me, that they may be one even as We are one: I in them and You in Me, that they may be perfect in unity, and that the world may know that You have sent Me, and have loved them as You have loved Me.
>
> —JOHN 17:20–23

Jesus prayed that we would be one with one another and with Him "even as We are one" (v. 22). In other words, we are to experience the same intimacy in this fellowship that the Father and the Son experience. In what ways are the Father and the Son in union with each other? Imagine how the Father looks at Jesus. That total acceptance and absolute love are intense—pure adoration—and it is the Holy Spirit who helps us connect to and experience this love relationship. The love the Father has for the Son is the same love He has for us. We are one just as they are one. We have been welcomed into the beautiful and intense fellowship of the Trinity. Not only that, but the Son also takes the glory the Father has given Him and shares it with us. You'll hear people say that God does not share His glory with others, and that's true in the sense that He will not let false gods share in it (Isa. 42:8; 48:11). But in the fellowship of the Trinity glory is shared all around. Miracles are a manifestation of God's glory. As His body we are able to partner with the Holy Spirit in seeing His glory revealed on earth. We get to be part of that. The same love that overflows among the Father, Son, and Spirit has been freely given to us, and the glory of the Son is shared. We are insiders in the deepest, most intense, most intimate relationship ever known.

You can tell when you're with someone who feels absolutely loved and accepted, can't you? People who are bathed in love just radiate. They are completely comfortable in their own skin because they know they will always be accepted. And they are able to love freely because they are so secure and unafraid of being rejected. If you've never experienced that, you can. There's a group that will never reject you. The Father, Son, and Spirit want to give you that feeling of belonging, and what they offer is amplified far beyond what any human being can give you. We looked at Paul's prayer in Ephesians 1, but two chapters later we see his prayer for us to be "rooted and grounded" in this unimaginable love. Paul asks that we would be strengthened in our inward being in order to experience this extreme kind of love—that we would know "the breadth and length and depth and height" of His love (Eph. 3:17–18). The wording of the next verse is quite remarkable: "to know the love of Christ which surpasses knowledge" (Eph. 3:19) How is it possible to know something that surpasses knowledge? One of the roles of the Spirit is to reveal the nature of this love to us that it might become our experience. God actually enables us to know what is humanly incomprehensible!

If you're ever feeling a deficit of love, the Holy Spirit is there to help you (Eph. 3:14–21). He sheds His love "abroad in our hearts" (Rom. 5:5), and He gives us access to God's love for other people. Just ask Him. I shared earlier that I wasn't even sure it was OK to talk to the Spirit. He enabled me to speak in tongues when I received the baptism of the Holy Spirit, and I was thankful for that. But it took some time to be comfortable with speaking directly to Him. However, once I began to acknowledge Him, He began to show up in extraordinary ways. I could ask Him to teach me about anything, or to comfort me when I needed comforting, or to set me free from any thought or problem that was bothering me. I learned how much He wanted to satisfy me with Himself. I realized how much I had been missing and wanted to talk with Him even more.

So the heart of God is not for us to walk alone and pray as though we are confined to earth and pressing through to try to get to Him. He wants us to engage with His Holy Spirit here and now, understanding that we don't have to strain to do it. If we just rest in Him and recognize His great love for us, acknowledge His presence, and look to Him for help, He will open the eyes of our hearts. And He will reveal Himself in greater and greater ways.

That's the beautiful ministry of the Holy Spirit. The rest

of this book will explore more specifically how He ministers in us and through us, but His ministry will always reflect His nature. He is kind, loving, jealous to be the one you turn to in times of need, always revealing the love of the Father and the Son, gently and patiently helping you learn how to have a conversation with Him and respond to Him, and ready to teach and encourage and empower you. And He is always, always with you.

Chapter 3

THE HOLY SPIRIT REVEALS
OUR IDENTITY AND DESTINY

WAS ON THE floor during a worship service years ago, touched by the Spirit and weeping in His presence. I had been hungry for Him and searching for answers. I struggled with condemnation, aware of my failings and imperfect behavior. Each time I sinned by having a wrong attitude or not demonstrating the fruit of the Spirit affirmed my sense of condemnation and my belief that, although God was love, He was probably loving me only because He had to! I assumed God was constantly disappointed in and frustrated with me. As I lay there crying, I turned my head and opened my eyes and had a vision of Jesus's face. He didn't look disappointed at all. His eyes were full of joy and love, so affectionate and soft. It was as if He were head over heels in love with me. It was overwhelming. What I saw was the opposite of what I believed to be true. God was looking at me with tender affection and without any sense of disapproval.

I had not experienced His kindness so clearly before. I had been trying hard to please Him but could not believe He would ever fully approve of me. That's one of the enemy's most deadly traps: no matter how hard you try, it's never enough. But the eyes of Jesus, so soft and full of love, changed my perception. God wasn't down on me for failing; He was deeply in love with me. He wanted me to see myself as He sees me so I could enjoy being with Him.

One of the Holy Spirit's greatest blessings is revealing the gaze of the Father and the Son to us. Not only does He reveal to us our acceptance in the family of God and invite us into fellowship, but He also helps us understand our identity in God. In that place of absolute joy in His presence we begin to see God's goodness, not as a theological belief about God but as certain knowledge in the depths of our hearts. When that gaze becomes real to us, we begin to know who He is and what He thinks about us, and we begin to understand who we are. Our identity comes from Him.

Too many people try to define themselves by their perceptions of themselves or by the opinions of others. That's why there are so many who are addicted to affirmation and spend their lives trying to measure up to what other people think. When the Spirit opens our eyes to how God really sees us, we realize we don't have to try to measure up anymore. Jesus has already measured up for us. His blood has already taken care of every way in which we've fallen short, and the Holy Spirit empowers us to live from His holiness. All the striving is out of the way, and God sees us as His beloved sons and daughters, the apples of His eye. We find ourselves in Him.

This is why I speak so often about the apostolic prayers. For example, Paul's great prayer for the Ephesians and for us was that we would have eyes to see who God is in order to understand who we are as people made in His image (Eph. 1:15–21). He prayed we would know the hope of our calling, understand that we are God's invaluable inheritance on earth, and understand the greatness of the power we have available to us. Ephesians 3 relates to God's desire for us to really know that Christ now lives in us and His longing that we would ask the Spirit for help in grasping the fullness of every dimension of His love so that we can be continually overflowing with all the fullness of who He is. I once prayed the apostolic prayers from Ephesians 1:15–21 and Ephesians 3:14–21 every day for three months, believing I would receive what I was asking for because I knew I could have whatever I asked for according to the will of God. I needed to see and know the Lord and experience His love. I had to have His perfect love cast out all my insecurities. I needed supernatural revelation of the truth that it was "no longer I who [lived], but Christ who [lived] in me" (Gal. 2:20). I knew that's where my identity and my destiny had to flow from.

As I prayed these prayers in faith, knowing these things were God's will for me because they were in His Word, I began to see as I had never seen before. I began to let go and let God love me, believing that He actually wanted to love me. The Word of God showed me that whenever I approached the Father, even with the littlest of faith, He was always running toward me with joy, just as the father of the prodigal son did toward his son (Luke 15:20). I began to believe that God the Father not only accepted me; He celebrated me. He let me see the look in His eyes when He gazed at me. I strongly encourage you to pray the prayers in Ephesians 1 and 3 and believe that this is how

God sees you. He wants to convince you that Jesus's sacrifice has made you clean and given you a new heart and mind. He wants you to know that He's delighted that you have stepped toward Him. There is no frustration in His gaze. It's pure delight. He is so pleased that you've come.

As the Spirit opens your eyes to how God sees you, His gaze will transform you. His perfect love will cast out all your fear (1 John 4:18). I can remember singing worship songs in my heart to Him one morning when He began singing songs to me, through me. His presence was so strong and the words coming out of my mouth were so beautiful that I could hardly move or breathe. They were words of passionate love—from me to Him and from Him to me. His heart was for me to know His love completely and be overwhelmed. We are all invited to experience moments such as this.

That's His heart for you too, and the Holy Spirit wants to reveal it to you. When you look at Him, He wants you to see Him looking back at you with pure delight in His eyes. He thinks you are beautiful. You need to believe that. You need to begin to see yourself the way He does. It's the only way you will be able to live out your identity and fulfill the destiny He has prepared for you. We are called to love one another, but we can't give what we haven't received. Scripture tells us to love one another as we love ourselves (James 2:8). We can only love people to the level that we love ourselves, so we must believe, receive, and come into agreement with the love God has for us.

There's a story by Brother Yun in his book *The Heavenly Man* that I often tell. During his time of imprisonment in China, Christians in prison were not allowed to talk to

one another, not even to say a few words of encouragement. They drew strength from one another by making
eye contact. The gaze itself would renew them, even when
everything else going on in their lives was disheartening.

That's what the Holy Spirit does for us. He gazes into
our eyes, and He enlightens the eyes of our hearts so we
are encouraged, strengthened, and filled with His love and
peace. As we gaze at Him, we begin to know who we actually are.

When you have been born again through faith in the
Son of God, exchanging your sin for His righteousness,
your nature for His new nature, your life for His life, "it
is no longer [you] who live, but Christ who lives in [you]"
(Gal. 2:20). Every day we have a choice to reckon ourselves
dead to ourselves and alive to Christ (Rom. 6:11). I do
this by deliberately taking captive any thought that does
not line up with what God thinks about me as a forgiven,
born-again believer. Every day we have the freedom to
choose whether we identify ourselves by our emotions or
by faith. If you feel condemned, the Holy Spirit wants to
remind you that as you have repented, He is faithful and
just to forgive you. If you feel powerless, He wants to stir
up your faith to believe that the same power that raised
Christ from the dead is now available to you.

God is love. The Holy Spirit wants you to know His love
so you will believe and manifest His love. Since God is love
and love is patient and kind, if you believe it is Christ who
lives in you, then you can believe that you are kind. As a
man "thinks in his heart, so is he" (Prov. 23:7). You are
patient, kind, and long-suffering, and you keep no record

of wrongs because you have been restored to the image of God. The Holy Spirit will remind you of that. Your identity is not in what you have or haven't done; it's in Him and what He has done. His opinion of you is the only one that matters, and it is extremely empowering.

You Are a Reflection of Glory

In the introduction I wrote about how we see ourselves as faint reflections of the true glory, but this perception of ourselves is a huge understatement. God has not offered us partial promises or hints of fulfillment. His purposes are much bigger than that. So why aren't many of us experiencing His fullness to the degree that we would like? Because the eyes of our understanding are not yet as open as they could be. When we really understand who God is, we begin to recognize who *we* are. Our true identity is in Him. Revelation about Him leads to revelation about ourselves. We gaze at Him and become "transformed into the same image," losing our misperceptions about being weak humans who can't get it right (2 Cor. 3:18). We begin to see that Christ really is "the hope of glory" living within us (Col. 1:27). We step into the reality of our true selves.

The Holy Spirit is waiting for us to respond to His invitation to enter into this reality. He wants that for our own sake, but He also wants it for the sake of the people around us. The more we understand who we are in Christ, the more we can show the world who God is in us. That's why Jesus is "the hope of glory" (Col. 1:27). This is what the world is waiting for. It needs us to live in the fullness of His promises.

The Holy Spirit walks with us to remind us of the reality

that we are thoroughly loved and accepted. He enables us to enter into the intense love of the Trinity. The negative self-image so many of us have had is a lie. No matter what we think of ourselves, the Holy Spirit wants to open our eyes to how thoroughly loved and adored we are.

That's a life-changing truth. Why? Because we all live out of the identity we see for ourselves. I'll talk about that more in the coming chapters, but you will almost always fulfill the vision you have of yourself. If you see yourself as a pitiful sinner who can't ever get things right, that's the identity you will probably live out. But if you see yourself as someone who has been radically redeemed and restored, a precious child of God in whom the Father delights, you will walk out that identity instead. We become what we behold (2 Cor. 3:18). When you are being convinced daily by the Holy Spirit of how much God values you, you won't try to get your value from other people's opinions; you will already know you are as accepted as you ever can be. You will live out of the assumption that you are loved, and that will enable you to love others freely and generously without the need to prove anything to them or hold anything against them. The ministry of the Holy Spirit will rid your life of that sense of rejection you used to feel. Then you are free to live out your destiny without anything holding you back.

The Spirit and the Word

One of the works of the Holy Spirit is to revive us personally and corporately. What does revival look like? I've been having that conversation with a lot of people lately because I really want to know, and I'm not sure we've completely figured it out yet. I've studied revivals and am hungry for God to do something really big, but I want to make sure I know how to partner with Him in it. I believe revival is a work of the Holy Spirit, and it begins on the inside and will work its way outward in glorious ways. And one of the ways it begins to work on the inside is by the Spirit's meeting us every day through His Word. As we feast on His voice in Scripture, He reminds us of what we look like and manifests His fruit in us.

James says if you're a hearer, and not a doer, of the Word, you're like a person who has looked in the mirror and then walked away and forgotten what he looks like (James 1:22–24). God isn't saying, "You pathetic people, why can't you try harder?" The point isn't to make you feel guilty for not living up to some standard. If you're not actually doing what you have seen in the Word and manifesting the fullness of Jesus with the fruit of His Spirit in miracles and power, He doesn't condemn you. The point is to help you realize what an amazing opportunity you are missing because you've forgotten what you look like.

I believe a big part of revival is the Holy Spirit's awakening believers to the truth of who they really are. We look for the outcome—the miracles and glory—but it also is in the daily devotional life. In fact, it has to happen there first. Christian character grows within as we persevere—perseverance "produces character, and character produces hope. And hope does not disappoint" (Rom. 5:4–5). If we deliberately lean into Him and don't shrivel up when the going gets tough but instead allow the Word to root us deeply in Him, we produce much fruit (John 15:7–8). In other words, if we remember who we are in Christ and don't give up, we win.

I enjoy studying whole books of scripture and listening to an audio Bible because reading and hearing the Word in sections keeps me from just picking and choosing the parts I like. But I also like to ask the Spirit for other places to read sometimes. I don't want to be so regimented in my study that I miss something He wants to say. Any way you can, it's good to let the Word dwell in you richly so you remember who you are and can bear beautiful fruit.

We need supernatural help to understand God's love because it's beyond human comprehension. That's why I strongly encourage people to pray the Bible. When you pray the Word of God, you can know you are praying according to His will. You can pray anything you like, of course; He loves to hear your voice. But it's very powerful to include in your prayers some scriptural prayers. I've mentioned several already, including Paul's prayers for wisdom and revelation, so you can know the hope of your calling, the riches of the glory of His inheritance in the saints, and the surpassing power available to those who believe. That's not just a little bit of power, by the way. It's the same power that raised Jesus from the dead. The Holy Spirit wants you to wake up to that so you will recognize what you carry. As you do, you begin to manifest Him in the earth.

I believe it is so important to feast on God's Word and make it a daily habit. When we read the Word, aware that the Holy Spirit is sitting with us, believing in Him to help us understand and receive revelation, we are fellowshipping with God Himself. It is a vital way to fellowship with the

Holy Spirit, and when we fellowship daily with the Holy Spirit and the Word, we maintain personal revival. I have a journal to record passages that speak to me, which helps me value what the Holy Spirit is saying and steward it in my life. Tom and I like to listen to an audio Bible every night as we go to sleep. We set a sleep timer on it, and even if we fall asleep before it ends, we're still receiving it. We just want to soak in it. Even if you don't have a lot of time, a little bit each day makes a tremendous difference. Read the Word. Listen to it, talk about it, take notes, and feed your spirit. It's like the daily manna that fell from heaven in the wilderness. The Israelites had to go and pick it up, but it was just there waiting for them. The Holy Spirit speaks through God's Word to remind you of who you are and what you carry.

Sometimes we get phone calls from people who say, "I need to speak to Pastor Katherine. Only Pastor Katherine will do." I feel sad sometimes because I feel they have their eyes on me instead of on God. The Holy Spirit wants to help them. I know it's important for members of the church to be able to seek help from one another, but the Holy Spirit is the only One who can carry you. No one else can fully satisfy your need and tell you who you are. You'll burn out friend after friend if you haven't learned to turn to God, the counsel of His Word, and the comfort of His Spirit when you're desperate, needy, and thirsty for edification, affirmation, and affection. He is always there to say, "I'm so glad you asked!"

The Holy Spirit doesn't just give you these things in small measure. He will fill you with the truth abundantly, causing His Word and His whispers to come alive in your heart. So many people are waiting for the perfect man or woman to "complete" them, but there's only one perfect person who can do that. Don't put that kind of pressure on a husband or a wife or a friend. If you're depending on someone else to make you feel OK about yourself or to tell you who you are, you're in a losing battle. That's not what he or she is there for. Enjoy the person for who he or she is, but turn to the Holy Spirit to have your needs filled. Only He knows how to affirm you in a way that satisfies that deep longing. Others can encourage, but they won't ever be able to fully satisfy you as He can.

The Holy Spirit not only wants to comfort you with kind words; He also wants you to believe what the Father says about you. If we only *hear* the Holy Spirit's words but fail to receive them, we deceive ourselves. For example, you can know as a concept that "it is no longer [you] who live, but Christ who lives in [you]," as Gal. 2:20 says, but when you actually believe that, you will be excited for the next person you meet!

The Holy Spirit is here to help you understand that you have been redeemed back to your original design. But as one created in the image of God, you also have the freedom to choose. Every day we can choose to walk by faith in the truth of our new identity or to yield to the temptation of being conformed to the pattern of the world (Rom. 12:1–2). Praise God—if we sin, we can repent and know that Christ's mercy is available. But we must put our faith in His forgiveness and believe we are righteous through His grace because "without faith it is impossible to please God" (Heb. 11:6). The Spirit gives us power to exercise self-control over our emotions so we can live out of the joy of knowing we are forgiven, clean, and free. Those who know and believe they are righteous are as bold as lions, but feeling and living in condemnation is simply unbelief. We must believe that when we confess our sin, He forgives us and makes us clean, and then live out of the freedom and joy of that truth. Christ in you wants to be the light of the world, and the Holy Spirit wants to bring personal revival to you in order to empower you to live as He is in this world and make sure no unbelief limits your arising and shining!

Dreaming Your Destiny

The Holy Spirit uses the screen of our imagination to help us see what God is saying to us. Once we are secure in who we are, we are ready to do what He has designed us to do. He wants to write His ideas and purposes into us. There was a time when I had a calling to ministry and dreamed of preaching on a platform and seeing miracles taking place and people getting saved. At the time it didn't seem possible, but I realized God had invited me to dream with Him, to let the vision of His calling fill me and lead me into my destiny. If the Holy Spirit had not helped me see the truth of God's character, I would not have been able to hold on to that vision. Even though I couldn't see it in the natural realm, I could see Him. I knew who He was, and therefore I knew who I was called to be.

That's how the Spirit often speaks to us. He cultivates visions in our hearts and invites us to step into them. He uses the screen of our imagination as an interactive experience with Him so we can not only see the dreams He has planted within us but also step into them, walk around in them, declare them, believe them, and eventually see them manifest.

Begin to dream about what you want to do and about what God wants you to do. Ask Him to download His desires and purposes into your heart. Learn to recognize the divine invitations the Holy Spirit is offering you as He drops thoughts and ideas into your mind throughout the day. Pray in the Spirit. Deliberately declare His purposes and plans. Let your mind wonder about kingdom things. Ask questions about the kingdom: What will it be like when people are experiencing Jesus all the time? What will it look like when people are healed at the sound of His name? How will I affect the people around me when I'm overflowing with His peace and love and joy? How obvious is it going to be to others that "it is no longer I who live, but Christ who lives in me" (Gal. 2:20)? Now that I am a new creation, how do I respond to people? What will it be like for the people around me to experience Jesus?

If you envision any destiny that isn't primarily about loving God and being loved by Him, bring it back to that focus. Christ must be at the center of everything we do: "The testimony of Jesus is the spirit of prophecy" (Rev. 19:10). So if the nature and character of Jesus aren't at the heart of what we are envisioning for our destinies, we need to look more carefully to find Him.

Remember, Jesus is the answer. That means we can be confident that His plans for us are filled with hope and glorious destiny.

> Delight yourself in the LORD, and He will give you
> the desires of your heart.
>
> —PSALM 37:4

> Seek first the kingdom of God and His righteous-
> ness, and all these things shall be given to you.
>
> —MATTHEW 6:33

His heart is first and foremost for you to be fully preoccupied with Him, and only then for you to talk about what
He wants you to do for Him. Identity always comes before
destiny. It centers you on the glorious reality of who He
is and who you are in Him. Everything else you do in
life needs to come from that place of knowing Him and
resting in who He says you are.

That's how God called Gideon. God first spoke to who
Gideon was—a mighty warrior, even though Gideon was
terrified and acting like anything but a mighty warrior
(Judg. 6:12). As Gideon stepped into a vision of his true self,
God led him in a plan to deliver Israel. His identity had to
come before his destiny could be fulfilled. The same was
true of Peter. Jesus called him a rock at a time when Peter
was acting like anything but a rock (Matt. 16:18). But Peter
became a fearless preacher in the early church because Jesus
had called out his identity before leading him into his destiny.

You'll find that in your dreaming the Holy Spirit may
not give you a vision of your destiny before you really
understand your identity. He loves to inspire us with
vision. But He never wants to lead you into your calling
until you are secure in who you are. The revelation of your
destiny and your identity can come in any order, but the

experience of your identity has to come before you walk out your destiny. In fact, you will not be able to carry the weight of your destiny unless you know how deeply He loves you and you have learned to find your identity in Him. When we are rooted and grounded in the love that passes all our understanding we can confidently believe Him and boldly step into the plans He has for us.

This identity is already yours. You don't have to strive for it, but you do need to gaze at Him in order to see it. Look into the mirror of His face to discover who you are. You will find yourself in His eyes, the way He sees you. You will begin to grasp who Jesus is in you, "the hope of glory" (Col. 1:27). Your mind will begin to be filled with the Holy Spirit's thoughts. Look at the Song of Songs, and read it with the knowledge that Christ is speaking to you, His bride. Or read Ephesians, and use the truth of the Word as a launchpad for your faith to begin embracing the reality of His intense love for you. When you start to believe how loved you are, you will think and behave differently.

The Awakening

In the awakening that is going on right now, people are beginning to realize who they are as born-again believers. They are waking up to their freedom and taking hold of the promises God has given. The Holy Spirit is teaching us how to see our destinies and walk in them. He wants us to believe Him and wage war for the promises in faith (1 Tim. 1:18–19). I do that by declaring what He has revealed to me, whether it is a scripture He has highlighted to me as a promise, or a prophetic word or vision that He has given me. Over the years He has taught me to say what He is saying and in faith be happy about it before I've even received it. He then releases a joyful expectation. We can rest in Him and receive all that He is and all He wants to give us. As we do, our lives with Him will be strengthened, and the awakening will grow.

The greater works that we long for always come out of a place of understanding our identities in Christ. We *do* because we *are*. Many believers are out there trying to do in order to become something—to do ministry so they can please God, to attempt miracles so they can see themselves as powerful, and so on. But *being* always comes before *doing*. Our ministry flows out of our fellowship with the Holy Spirit, our power flows out of His empowerment, and our hope comes from the fact that it's Christ who lives within us. We don't do the works of the kingdom to become significant. We already are significant. It is out of that place of knowing Him and knowing who we are in Him that we are able to do the greater works.

Ask the Holy Spirit to fill your mind with truth and vision. Pray for Him to open your eyes to all that He has for you, and agree with it. Above all, find your identity in His love through your fellowship with the Holy Spirit, and everything you do will flow from that place. When you find your identity in Him, the Holy Spirit will work through you, and you will do more to manifest the glory of the kingdom.

Chapter 4

THE HOLY SPIRIT AND POWER

A s OFTEN AS possible, Tom and I go to the gym together. I spend a lot of my time on the treadmill and rowing machine, but Tom goes to the big weights after a short warm-up. He can lift some really intimidating-looking weights. Me, not so much. And I know it's not just a matter of technique. I could watch how he does it—how he holds his hands and positions his feet, how he breathes, and so on—and then try to imitate exactly what he does. But if I got underneath those weights and used all of Tom's techniques, nothing would happen. I wouldn't be able to lift anything as heavy as the weights he lifts. Why? Because the method isn't the issue. Power is.

It's very much the same with the Holy Spirit. We can say all the right prayers, make all the right declarations, know all the right theology, and quote all the right verses, but our method really isn't the issue. Unless we understand that power flows from the Holy Spirit, we can't move anything. Nothing shifts. Even when we know theologically how much we need Him, nothing changes until we learn to interact with Him relationally. Then power begins to flow.

Before He ascended, Jesus told His followers they would receive power when the Holy Spirit came upon them. "And you shall be My witnesses in Jerusalem, and in all Judea and Samaria, and to the ends of the earth" (Acts 1:8). Remember, He was enthusiastic about the fact that when He left the disciples, He would send the Spirit to them. He told them it was better for them that He went away (John 16:7). He wanted them to receive power they didn't already have, and it was power for a purpose—that they (and we) would be His witnesses to the ends of the earth. The Holy Spirit empowers us to carry this invitation for people to be connected to the One who loves them more than life. But we need to learn what it means to lean on Him and walk in that power. This is not a matter of our being strong; in fact, He enjoys being strong for us in the midst of our weakness (2 Cor. 12:9–10). But we need to know how, in our weakness, to rest in Him. When Paul writes, "I can do all things through Christ" (Phil. 4:13, NKJV), the word *through* actually implies being in a position of rest.[1] That doesn't always come naturally for us. Even after we receive the baptism of the Holy Spirit and fire, we still have a choice every day of whether to do things in our own strength or lean into His.

Years ago in Augusta, Georgia, I was in a meeting and praying fervently for someone to be healed, but nothing was happening. I heard the voice of the Holy Spirit as if He were tapping me on the shoulder. "Would you like some help?" He asked.

Suddenly I realized what I had been doing. "Yes. Thank You!" I told Him. "Please help me." As soon as I leaned into Him, people started falling under the power of God and being healed before they even got close to me. Today it is common in my meetings for people to receive miracles and healing by the power of the Holy Spirit before I even call out their problems because His presence has power. His ways are so much better than ours. It's His power that does the work. "Not by might nor by power, but by My Spirit" (Zech. 4:6).

As we learn what it means to be aware of the person of the Holy Spirit within us, life gets easier. I don't mean there are no longer any troubles; we've been assured there are troubles in this world. But Jesus also has assured us that He has "overcome the world" (John 16:33). We will experience hardship, but there is a huge difference between going against the grain and going with the flow. If you want to do things on your own, you are in for a hard road. But if you learn how to lean into the Spirit, He will comfort you in all your troubles. "Many are the afflictions of the righteous, but the LORD delivers him out of them all" (Ps. 34:19). The Holy Spirit wants to remind you of the words of Jesus and encourage you with the promises of Scripture. He wants to help you use the weapons of your warfare. He wants to fill your mouth with powerfully effective prayers. He longs to tangibly comfort you and love you in a way that no human could. And He will never leave you. He doesn't get annoyed and decide not to talk to you for a while. He is always there and ready to help the moment you look to Him.

The "immeasurable and unlimited and surpassing greatness" of the Holy Spirit's power, available to us who believe, flows from the One who raised Christ from the dead (Eph. 1:19, AMP). Miracles are not done by our power but by the power of God the Holy Spirit. It's all about Him. When the disciples got excited that demons were submitting to them, Jesus reminded them not to rejoice in that but in the fact that their names were written in heaven (Luke 10:20). Jesus was pointing to the fact that while the power of miracles is wonderful, we must never get caught up in the power itself but in the One who is Lord of all. Our lives are meant to be like funnels—engaging with the Holy Spirit and releasing His power on the earth. Just as the funnel has a wide opening at the top ready to receive, the believer primarily should be occupied with the wonder and worship of God. As the Holy Spirit enlightens us with the knowledge of Him, we realize that the hope of our calling, all our value, and the power that we are called to walk in flows from Him through us as if we are funnels. Our eyes must be enlightened to see in the Spirit in order to maintain a posture of humility, wonder, and awe and be effective funnels for the Holy Spirit's power.

Seeing in the Spirit

I was in a camp worship service when I was about twelve, and I was trying hard to worship. I had believed in God since I was a little girl—the whole message. I just didn't know what to do to worship God. We had been told in Sunday school not to hold our hands at half-mast. "That's dishonoring to Jesus," they said. "It needs to be all the way." I wanted to do everything right, so I tried to do that with worship too. I just didn't know how.

I got real with God one day—that's always a good policy,

by the way—and said, "Lord, I can't see You. It's really hard to sing to You when I can't see You and don't feel like I even know You." And right there in the midst of worship I was truly converted. The Holy Spirit revealed the Father and the Son to me. I could see with the eyes of my understanding. That's the only way I know how to explain it. He enlightened my sanctified imagination. I knew that I knew that I knew. I no longer felt I was worshipping a concept or an idea or somebody out there I couldn't see. I knew Him! I thought, "Oh, there You are!" I suddenly had a connection and a direction for my affection.

It's very hard to keep up a conversation if you can't see or sense anybody, and the Holy Spirit's power comes to reveal the reality of God and His love to us. I'm not saying you have to see a complete image of God in order to worship Him, of course. Some people "see" well in the spirit, and others aren't that visual. But God wants to give you a unique supernatural knowing. You also may see Him in different ways at different times. Jesus appeared in a different form on the road to Emmaus, and two disciples didn't recognize Him (Luke 24:13–16). You won't have just one picture. The Holy Spirit wants to reveal what God is like to you all the time, and His revelation is always fresh. There's always more about Him to discover. This is the Holy Spirit's power at work. It's wonderful.

I believe the Holy Spirit wants to engage our sanctified minds so we can see God on the screens of our imaginations. Some people get really nervous about that, as if our imaginations are some kind of intruder on our spiritual lives. But God gave us imagination for a reason. It's a gift that comes from Him. Our imaginations are neutral screens; the one who writes on them determines whether the thoughts are good or evil. We can write on them, the devil can write on them, or the Holy Spirit can write on them. It all depends on to whom we're yielding. If we yield to the Holy Spirit, He will help us see what God is saying to us. We see that in Scripture God took Abraham out to look at all the stars as an illustration of how many descendants He was going to give him and then told him to imagine all the sand on the seashore just to reiterate the point (Gen. 15:5; 22:17). He still does that with us. He wants to activate our sanctified imagination so we can begin to conceive His ideas, plans, and purposes.

We talk about this quite a bit in our prophetic school. Often in the Book of Daniel it says Daniel looked and saw (Dan. 12:5). Daniel just kept looking, and what he saw was breathtaking. He saw all the way to the end of the age. A lot of people have different thoughts go through their minds during worship: "I believe in God," "That's a great song," "How good to see my friend here," or "Yes, Lord, I love You." God loves when we come to worship Him, but if we come to look and see while we worship, and we look with an expectation that we will see, we will see a lot more than we do without really looking. God opens the eyes of those who are looking intently in faith. "He is a rewarder of those who diligently seek Him" (Heb. 11:6). The Holy Spirit is powerful and wants to take us into deeper levels and help us look with an expectation to see.

Jesus said the Father is looking for worshippers who worship "in spirit and truth" (John 4:24). The Holy Spirit helps us worship "in spirit and truth"; He reminds us that we are connected to God and what the Father and Jesus are like, and He shows us new things to help us go deeper in our relationship with Him. The Father is looking for worshippers who will engage with the Spirit as He reveals truth. It blesses His heart when our worship is a response to a revelation of His overwhelming love. All we need to do when we worship is ask in faith for the Holy Spirit to help us respond to God.

In doing that we have to look with an expectation to experience Him. If you don't believe He wants to enlighten your eyes in the knowledge of Him, you are unlikely to receive anything because God must be approached in faith. The Holy Spirit is always looking to reveal something fresh about God to us. He wants to take us into deeper and deeper encounters with Him by His power. If we surrender our minds to Him with an expectation that what He writes on the screens of our imaginations is from Him, He very often gives us visions about who He is and what He wants to do.

Every time I come to worship, I expect God to show me something, and it's rarely the same thing. I expect to see. Sometimes it's a picture on the screen of my imagination, sometimes it's just a sense, and sometimes it's some insight or revelation. But it's always something. When Peter and John saw the lame man at the temple gate called Beautiful and told him to look at them, he fixed his eyes on them "expecting to receive something" (Acts 3:4–5). That's how we ought to approach worship—in faith, expecting to get something and looking to receive the help the Holy Spirit has come to give us, as He is powerful and faithful toward His people.

His goal is to enlighten the eyes of our understanding so we get revelation of the hope of our calling and the riches of the glory of our inheritance. He wants not only to calm us, comfort us, give us peace, take away all our fears, and pour His love into us but also to reveal hope, destiny, and power. He has so much more for us than just survival; He wants to awaken us to a life that goes way beyond into all sorts of victories and exploits. He loves to restore our souls, making us "lie down in green pastures" (Ps. 23:2–3). But He also wants to lift us up so we sit in the presence of our enemies and eat a banquet (v. 5). He wants to bring each of us into a place where we have such holy boldness that we recognize nothing is impossible for God and "all things are possible" for those who believe in Him (Matt. 19:26; Mark 9:23). That's the kind of strengthening we can expect every time we worship.

Ezekiel knew how to engage with the Holy Spirit's power in his sanctified imagination. He had a vision by the rivers of Babylon that was intense and glorious. John had visions too when he was on the island of Patmos. He was "in the Spirit on the Lord's Day," having fellowship with the Comforter while he was in exile, divinely connected with the Godhead, and Jesus revealed Himself in stunning ways as the Lord invited him to "come up here" and see the throne room and things to come (Rev. 1:10; 4:1). Both Ezekiel and John were looking expectantly, and they saw. That's available to us too. "Ask, and it will be given to you" (Luke 11:9). We can expect the Holy Spirit to reveal Christ to us and anticipate His creativity in showing us who He is and what He is doing.

I used to be a choir conductor at church. It was during a time when I had been pursuing the Holy Spirit for more and learning how He speaks. One day as I was conducting during a worship service, I sensed the Holy Spirit saying, "Would you kneel?"

"I can't right now," I answered. "I'm conducting the choir."

"It would be good for you to kneel."

"I would be drawing attention to myself in front of the choir! But…OK…"

As my knee touched the platform, I was ushered into an encounter in the throne room that I did not know how to cope with. Overwhelmed, I pulled myself out of the encounter. I thought that if I'd allowed myself to stay there, I would have ended up prostrate on the floor, completely undone. I was afraid it would be inappropriate to let myself turn into jelly on the floor in front of the choir and the whole church. I didn't want to make a spectacle of myself! I was still overly concerned and controlled by fear. Praise God, I have now learned that His "perfect love casts out fear," and I never have to worry about trusting His leading (1 John 4:18). If I end up as jelly on the floor, I can trust that God has a wonderful plan. Following His leading is always the right choice. Fortunately God didn't say, "Well, I'm never going to help her again." This was an invitation, and I knew if I would continue to listen to His voice and not worry about what people thought—allowing His love to set me free from the fear of man and to take me deeper—I would have more encounters. And I have. In fact, I always expect to encounter God in worship. He has taken me into such beautiful encounters that it doesn't really matter to me anymore what anyone else thinks, which is a miracle! Today when we have church, I'm front and center every time. I'll kneel, dance, do whatever the Holy Spirit leads me to do.

I'm not suggesting that you should do things in corporate worship times that would be distracting or disruptive. If you ever feel led to do something that might distract other people from focusing on and worshipping God or that would usurp authority in the room, it would be good to question if you are hearing accurately. The Holy Spirit is the author of divine order. But His idea of power and order and our ideas are not necessarily the same.

Occasionally I've said, "Maybe not right now; I'll just do it in my mind." I'm being honest because I don't want anyone to think God pressures us or will leave us alone if we miss Him once. But most of the time I do exactly what I feel led to do because I've learned that obedience brings blessing. His ways are better than our ways. His invitation is always well worth whatever it costs us to say yes to it.

When I was in the early stages of breaking away from my fear of others' opinions, I was in a worship service in which the lights were down, and because I was still a bit worried about what people would think, I was grateful for the darkness. I felt safe. I was looking expecting to see, and I suddenly saw in the peripheral vision of my mind's eye a part of the eye of God. I turned to look, and it kept moving, so I kept looking to follow His face. Before I knew it, I was dancing. Both Tom and I were raised in churches that didn't do that; we were taught to be respectable. So when I realized that my turning to see God's face was actually making me dance, I laughed. "You pulled me into this!" I told Him. He hadn't been bothered by my reluctance. He never said, "Oh, that pathetic woman who's so afraid of people." He found a gentle and humorous way of bringing me out of my box, and I began to learn just to go with Him.

I think the Holy Spirit was smiling over that. He was helping me get over myself. He will help you get over yourself too if you will lean into Him. You'll be OK. He's with you. He wants to help you relax. He's kind—kinder than anyone you've ever experienced. And He isn't always wanting to have serious conversations with you. When you boldly approach the throne of grace, cleansed not by your own works but by your faith in the Son of God, He is happy to see you. He wants to talk to you and help you. He's the Father, the One who runs to you to wrap His arms around you, kiss you, encourage you, and empower you by the power of the Holy Spirit. You may feel like a hypocrite when you worship, but the Father is eager for you to come. The Holy Spirit will show you the Father's joy and help you get over your reluctance.

The Power of the Spirit

Another time I was ministering in a very conservative church, and I heard the Holy Spirit say, "Crunch, crunch." I knew He wanted me to say it out loud on the microphone. So I did. I said, "Crunch, crunch," just like I had heard.

A woman a few rows back gasped and said, "Excuse me! Excuse me!"

"Yes, ma'am?"

"My hip has been twisted for years. It went crunch, crunch when you said that, and I was healed!"

The Holy Spirit in all His gentleness is also more powerful than any of us have yet understood. One day when I was ministering, a man who had problems in his feet came forward for prayer. I went to pray for him, but before I could touch him, the power of the Holy Spirit rushed through me and caused him to fly backward several feet. As he did, the soles of his brand-new shoes blew off, and he was instantly healed!

On another occasion a lady relayed to me that she felt she was healed as I walked into the room without even knowing she needed healing or laying hands on her. She later told me she felt the presence of the Holy Spirit when I entered the room.

Another time someone called and asked me to go to the hospital. A man with severe lacerations on his head had been admitted to the intensive care unit. Although the doctors had tried to remove the mud and debris, the cuts were too deep, and his situation was critical. As we walked into the intensive care unit, I became aware of the presence of the Holy Spirit and in faith released His power for healing. The next day the nurses told us the most extraordinary story. Soon after we had left, mud and debris began to spurt out of the man's head all over the pillow, completely clearing out his wounds. The wounds then swiftly healed up, and the man came to church a few months later to testify of his remarkable healing.

These stories demonstrate the power of the Holy Spirit and His creativity, and they are available to all believers.

The Holy Spirit's Gifts

As we learn to see in the Spirit and partner with Him, we find we are uniquely gifted to work with Him in certain areas. Through His power He gives diverse spiritual gifts to manifest His ministry in us and through us. We each have different gifts because God has wired His body to be interdependent. You and I cannot experience everything we need from God without the gifts of other members of the body of Christ, and they cannot experience everything they need without us. No one person has the full range of gifts, but everyone has at least one (usually more) to offer. There are so many facets to who God is that He has chosen to manifest Himself uniquely through millions and millions of believers, each one contributing something to the entire body in his or her own particular way.

So it is very important to exercise your spiritual gifts and to receive from others as they exercise theirs. The Holy Spirit may empower you on the spot for specific tasks, sometimes outside your normal areas of gifting, but over time you will begin to recognize certain gifts that you are especially empowered to express. Others will recognize these gifts in you, and you will likely see more fruit in these areas than in other things you do. But there are no rigid categories here; the Holy Spirit can empower you for any task at any moment. Some miraculous signs, such as those listed in Mark 16:17–18, are not reserved only for those who have specific gifts. They are for everyone who believes. You'll see this with most gifts, in fact. Not everyone is an evangelist, but everyone will have opportunities to share their faith. Not everyone is a prophet, but everyone can hear God's voice and share it. So it's important to lean into whatever He is doing in you at any time, even as you focus on the specific gifts He has given you.

The New Testament mentions a variety of spiritual gifts, as in Romans 12:6–8 and 1 Corinthians 12:8–10, for example. These lists are not exhaustive, but they do give us a good idea of how the Holy Spirit works through believers. As you learn to partner with the Holy Spirit, three groupings, each with three gifts in them, may be of particular interest.

Revelatory gifts: words of wisdom, words of knowledge, and prophecy

Paul dealt quite a bit with prophecy in 1 Corinthians, urging believers to eagerly desire all the spiritual gifts but especially that they would prophesy (1 Cor. 14:1). He also mentioned words of knowledge and words of wisdom in 1 Corinthians 12:8. These three together reveal who Jesus is and what He is saying. These gifts are a manifestation of the Holy Spirit living within us, and they reflect the character of God, so these spiritual gifts will be bathed in love, joy, peace, patience, kindness, and so on (Gal. 5:22–23). But in the manifestation there will also be a revelation of who Jesus is for the recipient. So a mature prophetic word is often a combination of a word of knowledge, a prophecy, and a word of wisdom.

The Holy Spirit will never just give you a word of knowledge without pointing you to who Jesus is in the midst of that. For example, He will not say, "I see that you're having a really hard time," and leave it at that. The revelatory gifts have the character of Christ and reveal who Jesus is (Rev.

19:10). When Jesus walked the earth, He always manifested Himself as the answer to everyone who came to Him with a problem. He is love, and He is the answer. So these gifts have to work in combination with one another to fully testify of Jesus. Words of knowledge are signs and wonders and can be very exciting, but they are not just information. If you get a word of knowledge, keep looking for the prophecy that comes with it. A word of knowledge will tell you what the situation is, a prophecy will tell you what the Holy Spirit wants to do in that situation, and a word of wisdom will tell you how a person can apply this knowledge to the situation. They are three aspects of the same revelation, and they work very powerfully in combination.

We see this at work in the way Jesus ministered to the woman at the well in John 4. He spoke directly into her situation, telling her about the husbands she had had (vv. 17–18), which made her want to know who He was. That word of knowledge was an invitation for her to discover His nature. Then He gave her a word of prophecy about a shift in the worship landscape and how the Father was looking for those who would worship Him in spirit and in truth (vv. 21–24). The word of wisdom that follows is not clearly stated in this passage, but we can see it in the way Jesus identified who He is and how the woman applied that knowledge by telling everyone in the town about Him (vv. 26, 39–42). It was clear that He was not just giving her information but also was inviting her and her friends to come to Him and believe.

If we have a word of knowledge about someone needing healing, for example, it's an invitation for that person to discover Jesus as his or her healer. Sometimes you will get wisdom without knowing where it came from, and it seems like a supernatural download. That's the Holy Spirit helping you apply His revelation in specific situations. The fruit of these gifts is that they work together to demonstrate Jesus and invite people to experience Him.

Power gifts: faith, healings, and miracles

First Corinthians 12:9–10 mentions faith, healings, and miracles together, and I believe that is because they often work together powerfully just as knowledge, prophecy, and wisdom do. They are distinct, but they complement one another. Healings apply specifically to sickness, disease, injury, and any infirmity through which God wants to demonstrate His nature as healer (Exod. 15:26). Jesus told His disciples specifically that these are among the signs that would follow those who believe (Mark 16:15–18). So these gifts are not exclusive in any way; they are for *anyone* who believes. He sent the disciples out to "heal the sick, cleanse the lepers, raise the dead" (Matt. 10:8). These are signs of the kingdom of God and manifestations of who Jesus is. Like the revelatory gifts they lead people into an encounter with Christ.

As with all gifts these gifts flow as we are rooted and anchored in Christ. There is an especially clear connection between our being rooted in the love of Christ and the gift of faith because "faith...works through love" (Gal. 5:6). As we are "rooted and grounded" in the height, depth, width, and breadth of Christ's love, we will produce fruit (Eph. 3:17). As our roots grow deeper into the love of Christ, our faith and our fruit increase. It is no coincidence that this passage about being "rooted and grounded in love" is followed by a statement about how God does "exceedingly abundantly beyond all that we ask or imagine, according to the power that works in us" (v. 20).

When you know His love this way, you often feel a supernatural empowerment come upon you to believe for the impossible. You will find yourself making declarations or declaring prophecies that combine with healings and miracles to manifest the power and love of Jesus. I find the gift of faith operating in me most often when I am ministering in healings and miracles. Sometimes I just pray for people out of knowing that it's the will of God, and I'm responding in obedience. But other times I feel a specific empowerment to believe for a miracle—to pray for anyone who is deaf, for example. When I feel that gift of faith, I have a holy boldness to say, "Bring me someone with a deaf ear." It's not a word of knowledge but a gift of faith rising up, and I know God wants to do a miracle in that area.

A miracle can have to do with healing—the deaf hearing, the blind seeing, a limb growing out, and so on—but it's a broader category. The distinction between healings and miracles is not always clear. All healings are miracles, while not all miracles are healings, as when Jesus turned water into wine and multiplied food to feed thousands. The Holy Spirit gives faith for these kinds of miracles in all kinds of situations. But in all the gifts they have to be working in love. If we don't have love, we don't have anything (1 Cor. 13:1–3), and we don't experience much power. The Holy Spirit gives us love to be able to activate faith and minister with compassion to heal and walk in supernatural power. As believers we need to be expecting to move in miracles because Jesus gave us that invitation. We can move in even greater works than the ones He did during His ministry (John 14:12).

Recently as I was praying for healing, a lady came forward asking for prayer for a skin condition. She was a missionary to Thailand and was on furlough. I was praying just from faith that it was God's will to heal people. F. F. Bosworth said, "Faith begins where the will of God is known."[2] She said she felt two whirlwinds going through her body as I prayed. A couple of days later she returned to the doctor and was diagnosed with leukemia and a very serious liver condition. This woman and her husband continued to stand in faith, praying for complete healing. She went back to the doctor later for an MRI and blood tests, and when the results came back, everything was normal. The MRI shocked the doctors; they couldn't believe they were seeing this woman's liver because it was perfectly healthy. She was also completely healed of leukemia.[3]

God does all kinds of miracles in response to faith—the kind of faith that responds to what we know to be His will as well as the gift of faith that rises up at some moments when He wants to do something remarkable. The Bible says when Jesus turned the water into wine, it was the beginning of the manifestation of His glory (John 2:11). That's the focus of all His miracles. The Holy Spirit wants to give us revelation of the power we have in Him. We can expect to see these manifestations of His nature as we lean into Him.

Heavenly communication: discerning of spirits, tongues, and interpretation of tongues

We can be aware of the spiritual realm by the power of the Holy Spirit (1 Cor. 12:10). This is not limited to demonic activity, as some emphasize. We can also be discerning of ministering spirits, recognizing how the Holy Spirit is moving or being aware of angelic activity. We can ask the Holy Spirit to open our eyes as Elisha did for his servant, who then saw God's armies gathered around them to fight on their behalf (2 Kings 6:17). I often see that in healing meetings when I ask the Holy Spirit to show me where angels are ministering, and I'll see an angel standing with somebody God is touching and healing. Or I'll see angels and ask the Lord what He is wanting to do. The same applies to asking the Holy Spirit what He is doing and how He is moving.

Of course this applies to evil spirits too. I remember praying for someone during an altar call when the presence of the Holy Spirit was extremely strong and someone nearby had just been delivered. Demons were manifesting. We don't make a big fuss about that, but they do have to go. And as I prayed for this person, I could see clearly in the Spirit that a little demon was crouching beside him. I could hear it saying to itself, "If I stay very still, she might not see me," which I thought was pretty funny. I rebuked it in the name of Jesus, and it had to leave. As soon as demons know you can see them, they can't handle it, and they run.

Tongues and the interpretation of tongues also fall in this group because they involve speaking and hearing in heavenly languages as a communication bridge between the realms of heaven and earth. These are very exciting, empowering gifts, but we will discuss tongues much more extensively in chapter 10, so I will not go into depth here. The important thing to remember is that none of these gifts are out of reach. You can ask for them and expect to receive (Luke 11:9–13; Eph. 1:17–19). They are part of your inheritance. You can believe and expect that He will empower you for whatever He leads you to do.

When you received Jesus, you also received the Spirit. You already have Him. But there is still a clothing with power from on high, a baptism of fire that is available. Jesus breathed on the disciples, and they received the Spirit in John 20:22, but He still told them to wait in Jerusalem to receive power from above (Acts 1:4–5). He is in you, but there is still a need for Him to come upon you. You need a continual infilling of the Spirit to empower and enable you—the Holy Spirit within you and upon you. When you have that, you begin to operate in the gift of faith and minister not out of your own strength but out of His. And then you will radiate His power and glory.

Chapter 5

WALKING IN THE FRUIT
OF THE SPIRIT

I REMEMBER ONCE BEING in a prayer meeting when I was on the floor worshipping and praying, looking at the Lord with expectation, quite stressed about a few things that had happened that week. Sometimes people have the tendency just to go along with the flow of a church service, not really thinking about what they are doing. They are worshipping without engaging, enjoying the atmosphere but not much more. That's not what I was doing that day. My focus was on the Lord. I was concentrating on Him intently and anticipating His help. As I looked to Him, God showed me a vision of myself. I was sitting at a window, looking out at a beautiful garden on a summer's day. The Holy Spirit came and sat right beside me. He was relaxed, at ease. Then He just began to speak promises from Scripture that took away all my fear. "Ah, thank You for reminding me of that," I said. He gave me three verses, and one after the other everything I was worried about was covered. He just smiled at me, and the fact that He was at ease put me at ease. That's how fellowship with Him affects us. You begin to receive the peace that He carries just by being with Him.

Peace is part of the fruit of the Spirit, along with eight other traits listed in Galatians 5. This isn't a comprehensive list of the blessings He brings; the Holy Spirit's blessings can't be limited to just nine attributes. But this fruit is life-changing if we understand and apply what Scripture is saying about how we can live in them. We are called to walk in and manifest the fruit of the Spirit, and He freely gives it to us.

> Now the works of the flesh are revealed, which are these: adultery, sexual immorality, impurity, lewdness, idolatry, sorcery, hatred, strife, jealousy, rage, selfishness, dissensions, heresies, envy, murders, drunkenness, carousing, and the like. I warn you, as I previously warned you, that those who do such things shall not inherit the kingdom of God. But the fruit of the Spirit is love, joy, peace, patience, gentleness, goodness, faith, meekness, and self-control; against such there is no law. Those who are Christ's have crucified the flesh with its passions and lusts.
>
> —GALATIANS 5:19–24

The good news is that if you're born again and walking in fellowship with the Spirit, you don't desire those old acts of the flesh anymore. You have the mind of Christ, which includes His motives and desires. If the enemy comes and says to you, "You want this," all you need to do is look to the Holy Spirit and say, "Help me remember who I am and where I am. Ah, yes, Lord—as Jesus is, so am I in this world. Christ is now living in me. I have no need of those things anymore because what I have now is so much better. I belong to Jesus, and my sinful nature has been crucified with Him. Thank You, Holy Spirit, for Your help." He will help you remember those truths in times of need if you ask Him.

I know many Christians who beat themselves up for not living in the fruit of the Spirit, saying things such as, "I need more patience," or, "I should have more joy." Philippians says to "let everyone come to know your gentleness" (Phil. 4:5). That tells us that gentleness is a part of our character, and we have a choice to agree with and live out of it. Scripture doesn't say, "Try to be gentle." It says, "Let everyone come to know *your* gentleness" (emphasis added). By faith every day you need to reckon yourself dead to yourself and alive to the nature of Christ so you can live out of His nature. Christ manifests all the fruit of the Spirit, so as you walk by faith in what has happened through the cross and in fellowship with the Holy Spirit, you can also manifest the fruit of the Spirit.

Manifesting the Fruit of the Spirit

Just as I was put at ease in that vision of sitting at the window, when we fellowship with the Holy Spirit, we become more aware of Him and more intimate with Him, and we begin to actually experience His nature flowing through us. He wants us to have such an awareness of His presence that we see all the fruit modeled by Him, and as we spend time with Him, we manifest what we see in Him.

We connect with Him and His nature. God is love, and as we believe "it is no longer [we] who live, but Christ who lives in [us]," we don't have to try to be loving (Gal. 2:20). Instead we must believe we have become the very definition of love because that is who He is.

What you believe is what you will manifest. Believe you are kind because that is part of your new nature. Believe you are patient. You are peace, and everywhere you go, people are impacted by the supernatural peace you carry. Instead of believing yourself to be stressed, meditate on the truth of God's peace, which lives in you. As you calm and quiet your soul and deliberately begin to meditate on these truths, they will become part of your belief system. Instead of your having concepts you just mentally accept, the Holy Spirit wants to help you take these truths deep into your heart until they become the reality from which you live. Christ is your identity, and as you allow the Holy Spirit to reveal Christ to you, you become what you behold.

I often love to meditate on the words of God as I spend quiet time with the Holy Spirit. Now I am not talking about sitting in a yoga pose and chanting or emptying my mind in order to connect with the universe! Christian meditation is very different from that. We are disciplining our minds to focus on God's truth until it becomes part of our belief system. Psalm 131 talks about calming and quieting our souls, and Christian meditation can help with this.

Recently in worship I heard the Holy Spirit ask, "How much do you love Me?"

I knew enough to defer back to Him. "Please tell me."

He said, "You love Me with all your heart, all your

soul, and all your mind." That really blessed me because my answer would have been based on my recent performance and how much time I had or hadn't given Him in prayer. Instead the Lord was reminding me that I have His heart, His mind, and His motives. I could have taken that as just a sweet compliment, but the Holy Spirit wants to do more than compliment us. He wants us to believe, receive, and digest His words. He wants His words to become part of our identity. We need to steward them. So later I took time to meditate on what He said. It took effort to focus my thoughts on that for even a few seconds, as other thoughts kept intruding. But as I kept choosing to reject other thoughts and focus on these words, the intimacy of them helped me begin to connect more deeply with Him. Now I try to do the same with scriptures the Holy Spirit highlights to me in my daily reading and with His *rhema* words to me. I don't want to miss out on the fruit that God's Word wants to produce in my life, so by meditating on the Word of God with the Holy Spirit, I give Him the opportunity to cause the words to take root in my heart. As I take the time to experience His living words, they can then grow up into a tree of life that produces fruit.

That means whenever you're trying to manifest the fruit of the Spirit, He's saying, "Just come and sit in the window with Me. Spend time with Me. Digest My Word, and it will happen." As we abide in Him, we will produce much fruit (John 15:5). It doesn't happen because of good theology or training; it happens through intimacy. The Holy Spirit wants to help you connect with the Godhead in a supernatural, glorious fellowship. That's His specialty.

That's what He is here to do—to have intimate fellowship with us and to be involved in every aspect of our lives.

I have a really good relationship with my family. I think my husband and children understand me. Tom knows me well enough by now to pick up on many of my thought processes. Sometimes my children can see just what is going on in my emotions, and my daughters seem to know when, and question me if, I'm entertaining a troubling thought. When you live in the same house with people for years, you get to know one another really well. But no one is able to truly understand every single thing that goes on in this complex life of mine. My family can understand me to a degree, but the Holy Spirit completely knows and understands me all the time. In Him I am fully known (1 Cor. 13:12). He also knows how to help me. He's our ever-present help in time of need, and my time of need is all the time. When I look to the One who wants to provide for all my needs "according to His riches in glory," I'll get help all the time (Phil. 4:19). But if I struggle on my own, He is left to say, "I hope she looks at Me soon. Remember, I'm here. Look at the beautiful sky, the flowers....All of creation is declaring My goodness and pointing you to Me. Look, and I'll remind you that you don't have to walk alone." He knows every detail of where I am now and where He wants to take me. The Holy Spirit knows me, so He knows best how to remind me to reckon myself dead, but alive to Him. When I am focused on the truth that I have been set free from me—that "it is no longer I who live, but Christ who lives in me"—I can have faith to expect His fruit to manifest in my everyday life.

The Fruit of the Spirit

The fruit of the Spirit listed in Galatians 5 are primarily about attitudes and character. They are inward fruits. But the Spirit wants to help us be fruitful outwardly too. The night before His crucifixion Jesus told His disciples, "You did not choose Me, but I chose you, and appointed you, that you should go and bear fruit, and that your fruit should remain, that the Father may give you whatever you ask Him in My name" (John 15:16). This is not the only verse in which Jesus tied prayer and fruitfulness together. "I will do whatever you ask in My name" (John 14:13). And a little later He says:

> On that day you will ask Me nothing. Truly, truly I say to you, whatever you ask the Father in My name, He will give it to you. Until now you have asked nothing in My name. Ask, and you will receive, that your joy may be full. I have told you these things in proverbs. But the time is coming when I will no longer speak to you in proverbs, for I will speak to you plainly about the Father. On that day you will ask in My name. I am not saying to you that I shall ask the Father on your behalf. For the Father Himself loves you, because you have loved Me, and have believed that I came from God. I came from the Father and have come into the world. As I said, I am leaving the world and am going to the Father.
> —JOHN 16:23–28

What is Jesus saying? As He does throughout this entire section of Scripture—John 14 through 17 is filled with His last teachings before His crucifixion, including the promise of the Spirit—He is giving His followers a picture of the Trinity and how we connect to this fellowship. One of the most beautiful things about this intimate relationship is that it produces fruit. As with a human marriage this divine intimacy is a place where life is birthed and growth happens. Jesus is saying that in the midst of this fellowship the Father will do whatever we ask in Jesus's name. If I send one of our staff members to another one with a request, it isn't going to be turned down because the request is coming in my name—it is from me. In the same way when Jesus sends us to the Father with a request in His name, it's the same as if Jesus were asking. We're asking not as an outsider but as an insider—as one already seated within this intimate fellowship.

We've seen this already in John 17, Jesus's prayer for His disciples, in which He talks about the unity we have with Him and with one another—that it's the same kind of unity the Father and the Son have with each other.

> I do not pray for these alone, but also for those who will believe in Me through their word, that they may all be one, as You, Father, are in Me, and I in You. May they also be one in Us, that the world may believe that You have sent Me. I have given them the glory which You gave Me, that they may be one even as We are one: I in them and You in Me, that they may be perfect in unity, and that the world may know that You have sent Me, and have loved them as You have loved Me.
>
> —JOHN 17:20–23

Jesus is saying, "I want them to experience what it is to be in the center of Our affection—to live in complete unity with Us, not as people on the outside but as those in Our inner circle." This is the beautiful fellowship that the Spirit continually brings to our awareness, and if we live from this place, we enter into and experience the fruitfulness of the Trinity—the same fellowship that spoke light and life into being in the beginning.

The Inner Circle

I shared in the first chapter about my experience with cliques in high school. I think most people can relate to that situation. People tend to be very conscious of social groups throughout their lives, especially during high school. Many people feel anxiety about being included in the groups with which they want to associate. Most of us—even those who were popular with a certain crowd—get a few wounds of rejection along the way. When we're still carrying those wounds, every rejection or rebuff gets amplified, and we work even harder to get accepted. All sorts of issues, such as bitterness, rage, frustration, and perfectionism, come to the surface. We want to be good enough to disprove this deep sense of rejection we picked up a long time ago.

The beauty of the Holy Spirit is that He reminds us of the greater reality—that we are thoroughly loved and accepted as part of the heavenly family. He bears witness with our spirits that we are truly children of the Father and are already seated with Him in heavenly places, even while we are still physically on earth. The intense love each member of the Trinity has for each other is the same love they all have for you and me. I'm surrounded by it; it's in me, on me, and all around me. It's who I am. I'm not the ugly duckling I thought I was; I'm actually a swan! And so are you. No matter how you've been feeling in the world around you, the Spirit wants to show you that you're adored, you're accepted, you belong, you're beautiful, and you're always the apple of His eye.

When you actually start to believe this, things change. All of us inevitably live out the identity we have for ourselves. As you think in your heart, so are you (Prov. 23:7). If your identity as a beloved child of God sinks into your heart, you will no longer look at other people's opinions as statements of your worth. You'll live with an assumption— an absolutely true one—that you are already so loved that you are free to love others. Instead of expecting rejection from others, you'll be looking for opportunities to share the incredible privilege you've been given. That's the ministry of the Holy Spirit. He connects you to the happy place of intimate fellowship. His fruit not only benefits us but also blesses those around us. It's absolutely delightful.

The Spirit wants to take you deeper into this inner circle of fellowship, where lives flourish and fruit grows. *You can have as much of God as you want.* You can be as intimate with Him as you want. He won't get offended when you don't spend much time with Him, but He will continue to draw you closer. He's saying, "I've got more to show you. I want you to interact with Me as a friend. I want to share My heart with you and show you things to come." He stirs a hunger in our hearts for more. We long for greater revelation of our heart's true home. That's the Spirit crying out within our spirits for what our hearts really want: to over-flow with the love, joy, and peace of the Godhead.

That's the essence of the prayer we looked at in Ephesians 3—that the Spirit would strengthen you on the inside so you can have revelation of His great love for you, that you would know the height and depth and width and breadth of His love. We need supernatural strength to even be able to handle it. It's beyond what the human body and soul can manage. It's a divine invitation for something that goes beyond what is humanly possible. If you're satisfied with only a little bit, the Spirit will keep walking beside you, putting His arms around you and comforting you when you need comfort and counseling you when you need counsel. But He will continually stir you to realize you were created for more. He is very patient. Many of us go about for years preoccupied with this or that problem, concern, or goal for our lives. He isn't angry about that, but He is looking forward to the day when you say, "I want to know You more. I want to experience You more deeply."

If you were given a whole country to possess, it would be yours. But you wouldn't experience it unless you actually got out there and walked around in it, would you? In the same way you've been given the kingdom of God and the power of the Spirit. He has made His authority available to you through the blood of Jesus, and He wants you to know the hope of your calling. All that belongs to Him is yours. But you can't ever experience these things until you start walking around in them. He has all sorts of adventures for you to enjoy. He wants you to experience that wonderful feeling of being able to ask in His name and receive. As your fruitfulness increases, so will your joy.

Imagine being at a concert with someone really famous and wearing a badge that gives you access into all areas. You would feel pretty good about being able to go where other people couldn't, right? Or imagine being high up in government circles with security clearance that gives you access to highly sensitive information. Wouldn't you feel a bit privileged and want to take advantage of the opportunity? That sense of power and privilege is true for you in the realm of the Spirit. You have been given access to the power of God. The name of Jesus is like a badge that gives you clearance into areas that other people can't access. You don't have to strain to see the power of God released. You already have it! You can glory in that fact—not with arrogance about being better than others but with a deep sense of gratitude that you get to share His power and love with the world.

This is very happy news!

Into the Throne Room

The Holy Spirit is the voice that leads us. "Your ears shall hear a word behind you, saying, 'This is the way, walk in it,' whenever you turn to the right hand and when you turn to the left" (Isa. 30:21). He is always behind us, whispering in our ears. John experienced God's voice when he was exiled on the island of Patmos, only it wasn't a whisper. He was worshipping in the Spirit, and he heard a loud voice like a trumpet behind him. Jesus told him to write whatever he saw and send it to the seven churches. So John turned to see the voice behind him—more confirmation that God is visual and speaks to us on the projector screens of our minds—and saw seven gold lamp stands and the Son of Man, dazzling in His glory, walking among them. The scene was so powerful and overwhelming that John fell at Jesus's feet as though dead. Jesus told him not to fear and touched him to lift him up. (See Revelation 1:11–18.)

After an extended spiritual tour of seven churches in Asia Minor, John had already seen into more eternal mysteries than most human beings have ever experienced. He could have said, "That was nice. Thank You, Lord. I'll be going now." But he didn't. He kept pressing in. He lingered in the presence of the Holy Spirit, looking expectantly for what God wanted to do. "After this I looked," the text tells us. The Holy Spirit always loves that, so He gave John more—an angelic invitation to "come up here" (Rev. 4:1). Immediately John was in the throne room of God seeing glorious things in unforgettable detail (Rev. 4:2).

We shouldn't expect the Spirit to repeat that same revelation to us in its entirety—it was unique to John and the story of Scripture—but He will definitely repeat the process with us. It's the same way He has always worked to draw people into the fellowship of the throne room. He stirs up our hunger, we look and listen with expectancy, He speaks, we respond, and—if we linger and continue to seek His revelation—we go deeper and higher into the intimacy of the Trinity. God now regularly takes me into the throne room during worship, and I have had many encounters with Him in heaven. It is where we are seated in Christ; it is our home, and we are invited to boldly approach the throne of God in faith. Every encounter brings me closer to

Him and gives me more revelation of the truth of the Word of God.

The fruit of the Spirit is a result of being intimately united in fellowship with Him. It isn't about doing the right things or performing well. He doesn't expect us to measure up to some impossible standard. Our fruitfulness is always relational, always a product of intimacy with the Father, Son, and Spirit. He grows His fruit into our hearts and spirits, and He grows His fruitfulness into our relationships and works as we ask the Father in the name of Jesus and receive what He has promised. This is entirely natural for those who know they are thoroughly loved and accepted into the divine fellowship. We rest in that happy place, and the Spirit bears the fruit of the kingdom in and through us.

Chapter 6

THE COMFORT AND COUNSEL OF THE SPIRIT

I WAS BLESSED WITH a day off recently, and it was delightful. I had been ministering every single day, so I was especially grateful for the break. I took a walk to talk with the Holy Spirit and was just enjoying my surroundings and the conversation. But I suddenly realized as He began to speak to me that my thoughts had been subconsciously filled with some worries. They were things I didn't have the right to be worried about. I heard His voice saying, "You were not made to think about these things."

I realized I had a default setting I didn't even know was there. In my inward conversation—that stream of thoughts we all have—I had developed a habit of worrying about things at a subconscious level. A lot of it was focused on what I needed, how this or that situation was going to work out, what if something bad happened to get in the way, and so on. As my mind began to relax, it was as if a pile of problems began to rise to the surface, and I was spending a lot of mental energy on how to fix them. I'd fallen into a trap of living in a place of worry.

Before this if someone had asked me if I was a worrier, I would have said no. I don't think I'm a worrier by nature. In fact, I think I'm a pretty happy person. But the Holy Spirit was showing me that my mind was defaulting back to an old human pattern of anxiety. Most of us have a tendency to ask, "What if?" about practically everything. That tendency had been lying beneath the surface of my conscious thoughts. The Holy Spirit brought it to the surface and gently reminded me that I wasn't made to think about such things. Worry is a thief of peace and joy.

When I was in Atlanta a few days later Tony Thompson, a fellow pastor who didn't know any of this, began to prophesy. "God says you weren't created to worry about anything," he said. "Your mind needs to be set on the miracles and the things He is going to do." That got my attention. It's so easy for our thinking to get filled up with questions: "How, God? When? Why did this happen? What's going to happen? What if…?" These questions can be relentless. There's a difference between living in anticipation of what God is going to do and living in anxiety about what might happen, and our questions tend to default to the latter if we're not intentional about taking worrying thoughts and exchanging them for His truth (2 Cor. 10:5). We're told to cast all our anxieties on the Lord because He cares for us (1 Pet. 5:7). Preoccupation with fears and concerns is not part of our design.

Perhaps you thought that life with the Holy Spirit was all about external fruit—seeing miracles, declaring God's words, and ministering in power. Those manifestations are certainly part of our relationship with Him. We are seeing more and more of them in our day. But if you want to walk in power outwardly, you will need to make some inward adjustments. The power of the Holy Spirit begins with His working inside us to bring us comfort. Personal, intimate fellowship with the Holy Spirit is the birthplace of demonstrated power.

I woke up unusually early one day recently, and as I struggled to get back to sleep, I heard the kind voice of the Holy Spirit invite me to come and have a cuddle with Him. I was out of bed like a shot. Who could resist an invitation like that? I had such a sweet time as we fellowshipped together while the rest of the house was asleep. When you have moments such as this with the Holy Spirit, you may be tempted to respond by reminding Him of what you've been struggling with and how unworthy you are. Thankfully nothing in the kingdom is based on your worthiness; it's all based on Jesus's worthiness and your faith in the fact that He lives within you. The Holy Spirit knows everything you're going through, and none of it is a hindrance to His love. He hasn't written you off. He says, "Come. Don't worry. Let Me give you My words; they will encourage and comfort you. Let Me help you remember who you are. Let Me show you who the Father is so your heart can settle down, and you can come into a place of peace and joy."

The Holy Spirit wants to comfort you and change your thinking and set you free so He can make room for you to think about something better. You are not called to think like a mere human; you're called to have the mind of Christ (1 Cor. 2:16). You are called to be "rooted and grounded in [God's] love" (Eph. 3:17). Knowing this love is the only way to be filled with "the fullness of God" (Eph. 3:19). Have you ever noticed that God does "exceedingly abundantly beyond" what we can ask or think, "according to the power that works in us" (Eph. 3:20)? It isn't just *for* us; it's *in* us. This kind of inner power comes from knowing and believing, not from going through the right motions. It begins in our hearts and minds. That takes some rearranging, or, as Paul put it, it requires the renewing of our minds (Rom. 12:2).

The Ministry of the Comforter

One of the words Jesus used for the Holy Spirit in John 14:16 is "Comforter" (KJV). That word is translated as helper, advocate, and counselor in other versions, but they all indicate that He comes alongside us to assist us, encourage us, and shape our thoughts. Sometimes we think of His role as comforter and assume that means He'll be there when we need comfort—that He does that only in special situations. But if His comfort was meant only for emergencies, Jesus would never have said it would be better for Him to go away so the Comforter could come (John 16:7, KJV). The Comforter does not want to be a last resort. He is not a crisis manager waiting for you to have emergencies to have a conversation with you. He is jealous to help you because He wants you to live and think completely differently from the way you did before. He has come that Christ might be manifested to you and through you.

One of the most important ways we can think differently is by casting our cares on Him, trusting Him to deal with them. James Graham, one of our church members, recently had an experience that illustrated just how strongly God wants us to let go of our worries. James had stage 4 cancer, and doctors weren't sure how much longer he had to live. We went to pray for him one morning; I had canceled a meeting to go pray with him. We came in and took photographs because we were believing for a really good report to come out of all the pain. The next night Jesus walked into his hospital room at midnight, and James had a seven-hour encounter with God. But during the entire seven hours, the Lord didn't say anything about cancer. James said he actually felt a little offended by that and finally said, "Lord, You haven't even mentioned cancer!"

"That's because it's irrelevant," God told him.

"Well, it's not irrelevant to me!"

Again, the Lord just said, "It's irrelevant."

James woke up entirely well. It's an amazing miracle and testimony. I thought about those words—"it's irrelevant"—as I took my walk on my day off and kept hearing the Lord say, "Your mind isn't made to think about these things." God really does want us to be able to cast our cares on Him and not pick them back up. Our worries really are irrelevant to us. Our minds were meant for better things.

The word Scripture uses for *cast* in 1 Peter 5:7 is *epiriptō*, and it implies a sudden motion, to fling with a quick toss.[1] It is like flicking something off your skin. It's not straining to pick up a huge boulder and trying to heave it away. It's a sudden reaction. The Lord wants us to realize that every time we have a what-if thought, our reflex should be to flick it away and say, "Not my problem." That's the counsel of the Comforter in our conversations with Him. When those thoughts come up, we toss them away.

This is what Paul was getting at in a well-known passage in Philippians:

> Rejoice in the Lord always. Again I will say, rejoice! Let everyone come to know your gentleness. The Lord is at hand. Be anxious for nothing, but in everything, by prayer and supplication with gratitude, make your requests known to God. And the peace of God, which surpasses all understanding, will protect your hearts and minds through Christ Jesus. Finally, brothers, whatever things are true, whatever things are honest, whatever things are just, whatever things are pure, whatever things are lovely, whatever things are of good report, if there is any virtue, and if there is any praise, think on these things. Do those things which you have both learned and received, and heard and seen in me, and the God of peace will be with you.
> —PHILIPPIANS 4:4–9

Rejoice. Don't be anxious about anything! Present your requests with gratitude. Think about good things. Then you will be filled with God's peace.

God is saying that if you have a circumstance in your life that causes fear or anxiety, don't just ignore it. Bring it to Him. Cast it onto Him quickly and deliberately, as if you're tossing it away. Giving thanks while doing this is vital because it demonstrates your trust in Him. When you ask with gratitude, you aren't worried about whether He will act on your behalf or not. You know He will. You can turn it over to Him, flicking off your worries in exchange for His peace.

What does that process look like? It can be a simple conversation: "Lord, I'm worried about this. I give You this concern. This is Your problem to deal with, and Your Word says You supply all our needs according to Your riches in glory. So thank You that I don't have to be worried about this anymore. I'm trusting You to do what You promised, and I know that You will turn this all around for Your glory and my good." If it's a sickness, you can acknowledge and declare that you are healed by His stripes and that you are no longer going to battle with it. "Lord, You say that no weapon formed against me shall prosper. You said You would satisfy me with long life and show me Your salvation. You said not to forget the benefits of the One who forgives all my sins and heals all my diseases. So Father, I call on You and declare that You are faithful, and I give You this concern and thank You for being my healer." Then you deliberately fix your thoughts on things that are pure and lovely and of good report. When the worries return, you flick them off, toss them away, resolving that they are not your problem anymore. Dismiss the what-ifs just as quickly as they come in.

This is more than just a good way to live; it's also a responsibility. Your mind was created to dream God's dreams, to envision His purposes, to pray them into reality, and to walk them out. Your mind is designed for the things of God. Why fill it up with unworthy clutter? You were made to carry the Son of God Himself into all the world—that goes back to the fruitfulness we talked about in the previous chapter—and if you're walking around with a mind filled with anxiety and worries, you're missing out on the dreams God wants to share with you. You can't be who you were meant to be if your mind and heart are weighed down with concerns.

God's desire is for us to embrace the comfort of the Comforter and the counsel of the Counselor. The point is not just for us to have a happy life, though His comfort and counsel will allow us to walk in beautiful, glorious peace, happy and free. The point is to be who we were created to be and be more aware of heavenly realities than of earthly realities. When you're filled with anxiety and worries, you can't see what He wants you to see. When our thoughts line up with His reality, our lives can begin to reflect this reality. We can't release His goodness if we are not aware of it. The Comforter comes to help you identify intruding thoughts and flick them off and then enables you to replace them with thoughts of Christ. He says, "Now let's think about what is really important." In the hospital the Comforter met James—who medically wasn't expected to wake up the next morning because of the cancer that filled his body and prevented his organs from working—and talked about future plans. If James's cancer was irrelevant to God, what would He say if you brought your worries and what-ifs to Him? I think He'd say, "I've got this. Let's talk about something happy now."

A New Way to Think

It's time to open our eyes and let the Holy Spirit help us embrace the mind of Christ. His mind-set is life and peace and freedom. Our worries are not. Without the Spirit, we will defer to the old patterns of thinking. We must consciously discipline our minds not to conform to old destructive patterns of human thinking. When we let the Holy Spirit help us, He reminds us that the normal human patterns do not apply. We are now citizens of heaven, seated with Christ in heavenly places, and therefore we don't have to be bound by earthly rules. For example, if a doctor gives a report that gives no hope, we know we have a higher truth. Our defaults can be changed because we are new creations. He reminds us of our new identities as members of the family of God. We have the mind of Christ! We are supernatural, eternal beings ruling and reigning with Him. We have been anointed as kings and priests to take His glory to the world. The glory of the Lord will cover the earth as the waters cover the sea because the carriers of His glory begin thinking His thoughts and aligning themselves with His purposes. The Comforter and Counselor will fill you with the right frame of mind to carry the glory of God, but only if you cast out the anxieties and worries that are junking up the space He wants to fill.

You will face opposition in this. The enemy will come in with all sorts of tactics. Thoughts such as "Who are you to say you have the mind of Christ when all these other issues are going on in your life?" or "Who are you to pray for the sick when you've got chronic back issues you can't deal with?" will plague you. When the enemy knocks on your door and tells you what a mess you're in, all you have to say is, "It is no longer I who live, but Christ who lives in me....I [choose] not to know anything...except Jesus Christ and Him crucified" (Gal. 2:20; 1 Cor. 2:2). You can tell your adversary that his accusations are irrelevant in light of God's truth. Then lean back into the Holy Spirit and ask for His help to fix your mind on whatever is good and true and lovely.

Instead of entertaining Satan's attempts to draw you into fear, what are some noble, true, and lovely thoughts you could fill your mind with? I think about what it will look like when I walk past people in wheelchairs, and they spontaneously jump up. I let my mind envision it because those are God's purposes that the Holy Spirit projects onto the screen of my imagination. I think about balls of fire going out over a congregation and healing and delivering people. I feel the power of prophetic words that set people free and call them into their destiny. I have the permission of the Holy Spirit and the Word to saturate my mind in these things. When I let my mind fall back into what I used to get worried and stressed about—and I have to be honest, this does still happen—I have to cast those cares onto the Lord. They are like the "little foxes that spoil the vineyards" (Songs 2:15).

I once had a dream that a tree was covered with web-like nests that had been made by large bats we call flying foxes in Australia. The tree looked stunted and awful. When I woke up, I talked to the Holy Spirit about it because the Counselor is always there to help us process these things. He said those flying foxes love to try to build nests in my mind. They are the cares of the world, the things that weigh me down and occupy my thoughts. Another name for flying foxes is fruit bats, and I thought, "Well, that fits. They eat fruit." Jesus said the cares of the world would make His people unfruitful (Matt. 13:22). So when I'm allowing concerns and worries to fill my thoughts, I'm actually letting them eat up the fruit God wants to manifest in and through me.

When people see you consumed with stress instead of being filled with the love, joy, peace, and patience of the Spirit, they probably aren't going to be attracted to what God is doing in your life. The bats are eating your fruit. But when people meet someone whose mind has been set on God, it is different. You live from the reality you most believe in. If you're beholding problems, that's what others will see. If you're living in fellowship with the Holy Spirit, setting your mind on things above and deliberately anticipating the goodness of God in your life, people are drawn to your different nature. Your fruit flourishes and can be seen by others.

What would happen if every believer prepared himself or herself before walking out of the bedroom in the morning? Most people look in the mirror to start their day. What if we looked in the mirror of His face? The earth is groaning and longing for the manifestation of the sons of God, but if the sons of God are distracted by little foxes and weighed down by anxieties and concerns, the world will miss out on the manifestation (Rom. 8:19). We can't afford to waste a moment of what Jesus has given us by filling our mental space with clutter. Christ in us is "the hope of glory" (Col. 1:27). Our minds need to be filled with Him and His thoughts.

I believe the Spirit wants to touch His people to deliver them from their worries. He wants to take you out of the place where you've been smothered in anxiety and fear and change your thinking. Don't feel shame about where your mind has been; there is no condemnation in His eyes. He is not looking at us thinking, "Those silly people. Why can't you just sort yourselves out?" He knows that the enemy comes to steal, kill, and destroy (John 10:10). Our joy, our peace, our dreams, and all our thought processes are under attack by the thief and the destroyer. But the Holy Spirit, our Comforter and Counselor, is giving us the awareness to respond with victory: "Ha-ha, God is for me! Who can be against me? All of those distractions are irrelevant!" We know God's plans are to prosper us and not to harm us, to give us a hope and a future (Jer. 29:11). We know He is faithful and worthy of our trust. The Spirit reminds us that our minds were not made for anxiety and fear. We don't need to be thinking about the things that stir up those worries. He is with you right now, in the room where you are, ready to help. He wants to encourage you, strengthen you, refresh you, and fill you with joy.

I was flying back home from Israel last year and had a moment of fear. Tom was sitting across the aisle from me, and I came under a spiritual attack; the fear was unlike anything I'd experienced before. I was afraid of the future, afraid of what could happen that was beyond my control, and it was overwhelming. I tried to fight it. I got out my Bible and started reading. I made declarations and even started to get some breakthrough. When we landed in Zurich, Switzerland, and walked down the gangway, I saw an advertisement on the wall. It was the only one there and was right in front of my face. It was for investment banking, but you wouldn't have known that at first because the words were so big: "Am I a good father?" I knew the Lord was speaking to me through that. "Am I a good Father? Then why are you worried?" He doesn't get angry when we're distracted by those little foxes, but He is very jealous to help. He wants to remind us that He is a good Father and that we have no reason to be worried.

Most of the time our worry comes from a desire to be in control. It's actually a form of idolatry because it's making something else out to be bigger than God. We put Him back in His proper place in our minds when we say, "You're a good Father. I'm going to trust in You. I refuse to worry about these things and choose to cast them on You. I have faith that You are a good Daddy." When the enemy or our own habits try to distract us with those what-ifs, all we need to do is ask the Holy Spirit to remind us that we have a good Father, and He will help us. He empowers us to set our minds on things above. The Holy Spirit fills our hearts with deliberate thanksgiving. The moment we start thanking God the enemy runs away. Sometimes I try to think of five things I'm thankful for, and even if they don't seem like monumental things at that moment, my gratitude makes a powerful weapon that immediately brings me into God's presence and helps me realize He is on my side. I thank Him that I have a house to live in and food to eat, that His plans for me are good, that His promises are true. Scripture says we "enter...His gates with thanksgiving" in our hearts (Ps. 100:4). Thanksgiving brings us into God's presence, and it is there that the oppression lifts, causing the enemy to flee.

The Holy Spirit wants us to live in a place of supernatural peace so we can make decisions from the mind of Christ, accessing the wisdom that comes from above. Sometimes when my heart is feeling overwhelmed with pressing issues that require decisions to be made, I close my eyes and consciously become aware of the presence of the Holy Spirit. I remind myself that I have the mind of Christ, and I allow the Holy Spirit to take me into the experience of that truth. James 3:17 says that "the wisdom that is from above is first pure, then peaceable, gentle, open to reason, full of mercy and good fruits, without partiality, and without hypocrisy." The Holy Spirit is the Spirit of wisdom, and He is available all the time to those who will calm and quiet their souls and lean into His wisdom by faith.

Freedom From Worries and Anxieties

Keeping our minds set on the Holy Spirit is so important. The Holy Spirit wants Jesus to be magnified and glorified in our thoughts. He wants our minds to be fixed on envisioning the hope and the future that He has in store for us so we can live in freedom, completely free from worries and anxieties. That's His territory, and He's rather jealous about it. Minds and hearts that are weighed down with concerns or criticisms are limited in what they can do. Minds and hearts that are free are able to demonstrate and receive His power.

Rest and freedom

One lady wrote me a lovely testimony recently after one of our services. She said as we were singing in the Spirit in tongues, I kept saying a phrase in Samoan: "Come rest in the bosom of the Father." Over and over again, apparently, I was saying that in a language I don't know. I was so excited to get that message, and I really do believe that's what the Holy Spirit is saying to us: "Come rest in the bosom of the Father." Fellowship with Him will always lead us to that place. Even if He has something specific for us to do, He wants us to do it from a place of resting in Him. We need to become like little children in our hearts and not trouble ourselves with weighty matters. We need to cease from worry and anxiety and simply trust.

One of my favorite psalms is Psalm 131:

> LORD, my heart is not haughty, nor my eyes lofty. Neither do I concern myself with great matters, nor with things too profound for me. Surely I have calmed and quieted my soul, like a weaned child with his mother; like a weaned child is my soul within me. O Israel, hope in the LORD from this time forth and forever.
>
> —PSALM 131, NKJV

I love this little psalm. This is mighty David, the warrior, the king, and he said, "Like a weaned child is my soul within me" (v. 2). I love the progression here. He realized that troubling himself with weighty matters would be thinking too much of himself and unfruitful, so he resolved not to burden himself with them. He didn't need to know how everything would work out. He refused to try to figure out the why, when, and how of what was happening in his life. He just didn't worry about those things. When someone wants to be god of his own little world, he has to concern himself with how it all needs to happen. But if David trusted God to be God, then his soul was calm and quiet. That's what David was doing. He disciplined his thoughts and deliberately came into rest. He realized he didn't belong to himself anymore. His life and his mind belonged to God. This is an Old Testament example of someone casting his cares on God and entering into rest by becoming like a little child.

I've wondered before how strong men would be able to relate to becoming like a child, but this was David, a mighty warrior. Godly, strong men are not self-sufficient. True strength comes from recognizing where our strength really comes from. It comes from hungering after God and resting in Him rather than striving for strength. David took captive any vain imaginations that would exalt themselves against the knowledge of God (2 Cor. 10:5). In this psalm he rejected the emotional weight of trying to figure out his circumstances and problems, humbled himself, and said, "These things are not my concern." That's where we find God's love and encouragement.

The Holy Spirit wants to help us walk in freedom. He offers Himself as a safe place to come in and rest, to find comfort and peace, and not to try to deal with all the things that are too big for us. He wants us to "rest in the bosom of the Father" like a child who just needs to have a cuddle with a parent. Deep down inside everyone desires that comfort in his or her spirit. The Holy Spirit wants to be our continuous comfort so we can have continuous peace and live in continuous rest—and continuously have the capacity to receive from Him.

The Holy Spirit and freedom

Freedom is a big deal. When you aren't living in freedom from worries and anxieties, you don't have the capacity to dream God's dreams, desire His desires, and receive the blueprints of His plans in your spirit. You're in survival mode, smothered with worries and concerns that preoccupy you. If the enemy can fill your mind with those, he will rob you of the peace and joy God wants for you. He will also rob the world around you because you were created to manifest Christ, not stress. The world needs you to be free.

That's why this is a much bigger issue than your own comfort and peace. The Comforter wants to comfort you all the time, of course; He enjoys doing that very much. He wants you to be free from heavy burdens because, contrary to the belief of some, there's nothing noble in carrying so much weight; it's actually pride. But the bigger picture is if you can learn to trust Him and let go of those concerns, living in freedom, you will overflow with the presence of God and walk in His love and power.

If you want to know how free you are, look at your

interaction with other people. That's a good indication. Many of them will even be able to help you identify what you spend the most time thinking about because what you think about will inevitably show on your face and come out of your mouth. Out of the heart the mouth speaks (Luke 6:45). If your default is to follow up every "Hi, how are you?" with a statement about your problems or some subdued response, that's a good sign that a soundtrack of worry is playing in your mind and occupying the space the Holy Spirit wants to fill. There's no condemnation for that; God isn't annoyed. But when you realize the worry is there, He is delighted to step in and help you with it. He will show you how to enter into true rest.

I think God often wants to say, "Can we talk about something else now?" He wants us to attach faith to the truth of what He says so we can move forward in freedom. In the Gospel of John there's a wonderful picture where John is leaning against Jesus at the Last Supper, where John could hear Jesus's heartbeat and know what Jesus was whispering (John 13:23). This is the same John who had a vision in Revelation and fell at Jesus's feet as though dead (Rev. 1:17). Awe and revelation do come from this kind of relationship at times. But in the moment of the Last Supper John simply leaned against Jesus and filled up on His love. God is looking for hearts that hunger for Him in the same way. He wants us to rid our minds of worries, drink deeply of the river of His pleasure, and fill up with the love that casts out all fear. If we're going to be preoccupied about something, why not that? Overdose on His love. Cry out for supernatural strength so you can truly comprehend the concept of Christ's dwelling in your heart by faith and can know the height and depth and width and breadth of His love and be filled to overflowing with His fullness (Eph. 3:16–19). Then you can overflow to the world around you. You can be an expression of the God who wants to do "exceedingly abundantly beyond all that we ask or imagine" (Eph. 3:20).

You are called to be an ambassador of hope. If the enemy is throwing affliction or trouble at you, there is good news. "Many are the afflictions of the righteous, but the LORD delivers him out of them all" (Ps. 34:19). If something in your world is harassing you—some pain, sickness, or adversity—you don't need to figure out what you're doing wrong. You can know that this is normal for the righteous. "Many are the afflictions of the righteous" messes up the theology of a lot of ministries of judgment—for instance, Job's friends don't know what to do with that, but you can take comfort in it. Yes, there are times when you reap what you sow, and it's important to walk in forgiveness and grace. But walking in forgiveness and grace does not require figuring everything out. That's not our responsibility. In order to be free in the Holy Spirit, we need to get out of the place of trying to be God and into the place of being the child on His lap.

At one point in the ministry of Jesus the message became so confrontational that people began to leave. Some who had followed Him decided not to walk with Him anymore. Like many of us they were tempted to throw in the towel when things got tough. Jesus turned to the twelve disciples and asked, "Do you also want to go away?" (John 6:67).

I love Peter's response: "Lord, to whom shall we go? You have the words of eternal life" (v. 68).

That's the bottom line. No, I can't figure it all out. Sometimes I don't understand what's happening in my life. But the bottom line is I trust Him. Where else am I going to go? I choose trust, and with the Holy Spirit's help I calm my soul and tell it to line up with what God's Word says.

I was so touched when I watched the movie *The Hiding Place* by seeing Betsie ten Boom's response to someone who challenged her faith in God while she was in the Nazi concentration camp. She was asked, "If God is real, why are you here?" Her response was amazing. She said, "When you know Him, you don't need to know why." I love that because there is a peace that passes understanding available to those who truly know the Holy Spirit. God is faithful and absolutely trustworthy. I can anchor myself in what the Word of God says and declare that these are the words of eternal life. I don't have to understand everything. I just know that He is truth. The Holy Spirit has come to reveal that truth, and knowing the truth sets me free.

Dream His Dreams

The Holy Spirit is inviting you to dream about what you want to do and what God wants you to do. He wants the screen of your imagination to be uncluttered and free to receive His desires and purposes. Ask Him for His desires. Pray in the Spirit with expectation that He will show you things you don't already know. Declare what He tells you. Envision what it will be like when people are healed, delivered, or filled with joy and peace because of the Spirit working within you. Think about how amazing it is for people to experience Jesus through you.

The enemy wants to smother you with oppression and fill your thoughts with the evil possibilities. God has given you the oil of joy in place of the spirit of heaviness. Take it. Don't refuse that gift. You have access to the thoughts of God, and His thoughts are always higher than yours. We access His thoughts by asking the Holy Spirit to show us what He is dreaming of doing through our lives. Far too many people have been hit with oppressive thoughts and are so familiar with them that they seem normal. The reality is that God's higher thoughts are now normal for you. He is switching your default from worry to worship, and this is when His dreams become your reality. I wrote in my first book, *Living in the Miraculous*, about the importance of responding to God's divine invitations and dreaming His dreams. This is vital to helping us live in the fullness of our God-given destiny.

You are responsible to cast your cares on the Lord; that's your responsibility as a carrier of His glory. It's imperative. This is how the world will see Him as His people rise and shine with His glory. All those oppressive thoughts are now none of your business. They are irrelevant—not your problem. Your job is to ask the Holy Spirit to reveal God's thoughts and dreams for your life and empower you to live them out for the benefit of the world around you. That is your inheritance and your portion—right now and forever—and what the world is waiting for.

Chapter 7

THE HOLY SPIRIT AND FORGIVENESS

I MET PASTOR PAUL Santos in Baltimore. This Brazilian minister is an amazing man with a very unusual story. Years ago when he was a pastor in the Caribbean, his min-istry was experiencing a lot of warfare, and unbeknownst to him he had developed a brain tumor. He was driving slowly down the street one day with his family and had a seizure and died. He was dead for six hours while his wife was interceding for him to be raised from the dead.

I asked Pastor Paul what happened during those six hours. He said he was in heaven and that it was amazingly beautiful. It was absolutely glorious. But finally the Lord told him, "Paul, you need to go."

"There's room for me here," he protested. "I could just lie down here and stay."

"Paul, you need to go home." As Paul was leaving, the Lord spoke again.

"Paul, what is forgiveness?"

Paul gave a theological answer, but the Lord asked again.

"Paul, what is forgiveness?" So Paul tried to elaborate a little more on the answer, and still the Lord asked again, "What is forgiveness, Paul?"

Paul thought he had already done everything he could to forgive everyone. He had been conceived in rape, his stepfather had abused him, and he was thrown out of his home as a young man when he gave his life to the Lord, so forgiveness had not come easily. But he really thought he had forgiven everyone for what they had done to him. So after the third time God asked, Paul answered, "You tell me."

That's a pretty smart answer anytime the Lord asks you a question. The Lord said, "Forgiveness is the ability to go on in life with the consequences of someone else's mistake without being hurt."

I love that, but when Paul first said it, I thought to myself, "Is that really possible?" It seems so far removed from our experience. But of course it's possible; all things are possible with Christ. In fact, this freedom from the pain of the past is what His message is all about. It's why the angels were able to declare peace on earth and goodwill toward men. Anyone who is filled with the Spirit now has access to a life full of peace that passes understanding—a supernatural peace that is independent of circumstances and situations. This kind of forgiveness takes the pain away.

It is a vital prerequisite for living a supernatural life. It opens up a life of abundance.

Hearts Made for Love

Hebrews tells us that without the shedding of blood there is no forgiveness of sin, and that the blood of bulls and goats and lambs is not enough to cleanse a person's conscience (Heb. 9:13–14, 22). So Jesus came for us as the perfect sacrifice and was crucified at the very time the Passover lambs were being slain. When He laid down His life, He atoned for our sins, but He did far more than that. He has dealt with everything that defined us as imperfect and made us brand new on the inside.

When you receive the Lamb of God as your Savior, you get a new nature by the power of the Holy Spirit. That's necessary because without perfect holiness you can't have fellowship with God. There is no fellowship between light and darkness, so we need the blood of the Lamb to give us Christ's righteousness. The only way we can partner with the Holy Spirit—or enter into the presence of God to have any sort of connection with Him at all -is by having a new identity. We exchange our sin for His righteousness, our crookedness for His magnificence, everything we are for everything He is. Then we can have unbroken fellowship with His Holy Spirit.

Not only is Jesus the Lamb who takes away the sins of the world, but He's also the Lion who rises up in power. And the same power with which the Holy Spirit raised Jesus from the grave—the power of the Lion of Judah, the all-conquering King who overcame sin and death and took the forces of darkness captive—now lives in you (Rom. 8:11).

As I was thinking about the power of Jesus's death and resurrection last Easter, it struck me how little sense it makes, humanly speaking. The essence of the gospel is that Jesus was made to be sin on our behalf, was separated from the Father (who turned His face away), and bore the sin of the world as He died. He became sin so we could become righteousness and have fellowship with the Holy Spirit (2 Cor. 5:21). It's very simple, but it requires faith to believe this because it doesn't make sense to humans. In fact, the human mind wants to make it more difficult. It doesn't seem right that anyone can just come to God and say, "I've sinned, and I need Your forgiveness. Have mercy on me, come into my life, and give me a new heart and a new life." That doesn't seem fair to us, so we make up other rules. But it really is that simple. The good news is we are saved by grace through faith (Eph. 2:8).

What caught my attention most as I was thinking about this was that Jesus was mocked and treated cruelly and brutally, even though He had never sinned, and yet He still could say, "Father, forgive them, for they know not what they do" (Luke 23:34). He had no hatred or anger. He was not defending Himself. He wasn't reviling them in return or fighting for His rights. He just released forgiveness. I am undone by the reality of this forgiveness and even more by the fact that this same forgiveness is available to us. The Holy Spirit empowers and teaches us to go and forgive others just as we have been forgiven (Col. 3:13).

As I've thought about how God defined forgiveness for Pastor Paul, I've sensed the Holy Spirit dealing with my own heart, particularly with regard to judgment. Forgiveness is an interesting subject and not one I fully understand. Scripture says that "mercy triumphs over judgment" (James 2:13), and it was Jesus's joy to become the One who was judged so we could be given mercy. He willingly did that for the joy set before Him. However, I don't think we always live in the full extent of that mercy. Instead we often live with pain beyond what we were created to experience. I don't mean to minimize trauma and pain; some people have experienced extremely traumatizing events that have created really deep wounds. These wounds cannot be easily dismissed. But the Holy Spirit's message of forgiveness and restoration is powerful enough even for the worst cases. Our hearts were made for love, not for judgment. Healing and peace are part of our inheritance and a major ministry of the Holy Spirit in our lives.

The world's view of forgiveness

We easily become conformed to the pattern of the world on the matter of forgiveness if we aren't feasting on the truth of God. The world's culture is quick to apply judgment, and the concept of forgiveness is quite foreign to many people. So this really does require a whole new way of thinking for believers. We have to let the Holy Spirit renew our minds so we can live in perfect peace, not pain, and fully enjoy the blessing of the kingdom.

This is something I'm still learning. I'm a new creation, the righteousness of God in Christ. I have His nature and His mind. That's wonderful. But how do I grow in understanding? How do I walk in a way that is pleasing to Him? How do I take captive every thought that exalts itself against the knowledge of Christ, who came to give us abundant life? How do I go deeper in the Spirit and grow into greater maturity? How do I live in His presence with an uncluttered heart and mind? How do I forgive others as Christ has forgiven me? These are questions with which the Holy Spirit wants to help.

The Bible tells us, "To be carnally minded is death, but to be spiritually minded is life and peace" (Rom. 8:6). That's beautiful—life and peace in the Spirit. And it's possible; otherwise we wouldn't be told to seek that. But many Christians don't spend the majority of their time thinking about things that are life and peace. There's no condemnation in that. I know how easy it is for the mind to get off on other things. But the Father longs for us to experience the fullness of abundant life. We were created for joy, and anything less comes from deception. When we relive pain unnecessarily, when we clutter our minds with judgments and allow our hearts to be poisoned with unforgiveness, we forfeit the joy we were designed to have and deprive the world of the love of Christ in us.

Judgment from unforgiveness

I recently had a dream about some bad experiences that happened a few years ago, and I woke up troubled. I hadn't thought about that time for a while, but the dream triggered memories about some people who had harmed me then, and I started thinking about what they had done: "That was so cruel. If they knew how much I was suffering, they wouldn't have done what they did. Maybe one day I can explain to them how mean and nasty that was." The Holy Spirit put His arm around me and said, "You know, Katherine, that's judgment."

I quickly realized He was right. I had gone from thinking what they did was wrong to thinking they were cruel. The first thought I had was focused on the action. We are supposed to discern right from wrong, and we are allowed to say when something is wrong. That isn't judgment. We can even confront someone for wrong behavior, so long as we do it with love. But the moment I take the next step and start assuming I know the motives of people's hearts, I step into judgment. I was no longer calling an action evil but calling a person evil, and that's very different. When we do this, we fill our hearts with things that are not meant to be there, and we build an offense that could come back to bite us. The devil will exploit that by reminding us of it, and if we engage in judgment each time it comes to mind, the pain will continue to recur. So I was really grateful when the Holy Spirit showed me I was judging. I thanked Him for letting me see and prayed for forgiveness for judging. I don't know if the individuals who hurt me had good motives or not, but that doesn't matter anymore. It isn't my place to be their judge, and I needed to be free from that false responsibility.

Judgment is not ours. The Holy Spirit wants to help us release people from our judgments, repent for when we have stood in the place of God, and ask for forgiveness. Then we are free to love our enemies and to overflow as the Holy Spirit continuously seeks to shed His love abroad in our hearts.

I believe part of keeping a clear conscience and walking in the Spirit is walking in humility. Pride in all its forms is dangerous, and judgment is a form of pride. It says, "I see what's wrong with you (and also what is *not* wrong with me)." And the next logical thought is, "I could fix that." Jesus called this looking at the speck in someone else's eye while ignoring the log in your own (Matt. 7:3). You can't see clearly when you have a log in your eye. But God is calling us to the kind of humility that does not apologize for who we are in Him but walks with respect and compassion toward others. I'm all for righteousness, and I'm not saying we should wink at sin. We're supposed to know the difference between right and wrong, and there are times when it is our responsibility to speak the truth in love. But a lot of people get very mixed up about that and speak the truth in pride and arrogance and with a desire to control, and that isn't how the Holy Spirit operates. He fills us with humility.

What forgiveness does for you

What do we have to lose by delighting in truth, walking in love, believing the best, showering grace and forgiveness on people, and seeing the good, the true, and the beautiful in others? The Holy Spirit empowers us to prophesy the heart of God for people, calling them into their God-given destiny. That's pure and peaceable, and it comes from a place of adoration of God and humility about ourselves, which go hand in hand.

I've had people approach me and say, "I need to apologize to you because I've held resentment against you for a long time." I'm sure that helps them feel better, but it doesn't do much for me. I realize Jesus said to go to your brother or sister to sort things out if you're making an offering and realize you have something against him or her (Matt. 5:23–24). He wanted people to see that their relationship with God was not independent of their relationship with others. I take that seriously because the fact is I'm bringing an offering of worship to the Lord every single day, and I don't want to come with unresolved conflict in the way. However, if going to another person will increase the feeling of conflict, resolve it another way. In order to maintain a clear conscience there are some things you will take to a brother or sister, but others you will take to God alone. You don't want to prolong conflict; you want to overcome it.

Tom and I have been married for twenty-five years, and our relationship gets sweeter as the days go by. We made a decision early on in our marriage not to let "the sun go down on [our] anger" (Eph. 4:26). In the early years we were still having some conversations at 3:00 a.m. because we didn't want to go to sleep before sorting things out. My heart can't be at peace when I have not done my best to be at peace with someone else, so that was a good practice for our marriage. I feel as if I need to do everything possible to live at peace with other people, and that begins at home.

I realize you can't always sort everything out with everyone. You will never be able to make everyone happy. God has not called us to be people-pleasers but to make peace with people as far as possible (Rom. 12:18). What I'm talking about is overcoming and walking in righteousness and peace rather than holding on to the resentment and bitterness that will eat you up inside. People-pleasing can increase resentment and bitterness because you appease others by freeing them from conflict while absorbing all the conflict yourself. Real peace comes from dealing with conflict in humility, apologizing without justifying anything you did wrong, forgiving and overlooking others' wrongs where necessary, and handing the pain over to God. Don't worry about what others will think of you. Be more concerned with walking in righteousness and peace than with other people's opinions. Make it your goal to exude kindness, radiate love, and walk in humility toward everyone through the supernatural strength of the Holy Spirit.

Jesus carries the sins of the world, so you don't have to. You were created for life and peace. The weapons of your warfare are mighty for the pulling down of strongholds, so there's no reason to be trapped in a life of pain. Yes, traumatic things happen in people's lives, and I am not minimizing that. I'm not suggesting you can live a life free from pain. Jesus was clear that there would be tribulation. As Scripture says, "Many are the afflictions of the righteous, but the LORD delivers him out of them all" (Ps. 34:19). But that doesn't mean we should take on anything more. Pain will happen, but there's no reason to inflict it on ourselves, nurse our wounds, rehearse our offenses, or figure out how to get people to understand that they have hurt us and punish them for it. We have to deliberately choose not to take on judgments that will steal our peace and cripple our ability to love others well. The Holy Spirit wants to counsel us to navigate the pain that comes against us in order to help us walk free and healed.

The Walls We Build

Judgments and offenses will affect your sense of peace and joy, but your attitude also has practical implications in your life. Say, for example, you go into work one day and find out that you didn't get a special project or promotion you were hoping for. It was given to someone else. That can be really painful. You can be honest about that. But the next step people often take is to start assigning motives. "My boss doesn't like me. I'm not appreciated for what I do around here. So-and-so must have been talking about me." You know where our minds can go. Before long you're carrying a grudge, you're discouraged, and you may even feel stuck where you are because you believe you will never be promoted. You may even be right, but assigning motives doesn't help. Remember, we reap what we sow, and we don't want to be reaping judgment (Gal. 6:7). Those judgments build up a wall inside you that makes interaction with the people you're judging really difficult. Outwardly you may be smiling, but people will sense something is wrong. Your eyes are the window of the soul, and they will tell on you. Out of the abundance of the heart the mouth speaks (Luke 6:45). Something will come out to somebody, and it will get around.

Now what if a few weeks later your boss wants to give you an even better position but now has the faint impression you don't like him very much or that you don't really enjoy working there? You've spoiled your chances by carrying around a judgment that you were never meant to carry. Not only have you been carrying around pain; you've missed out on opportunities to experience God's blessings in your life. You've created an inward environment that spills over into your outward environment and undermines your relationships and experiences. The Holy Spirit wants so much better for you.

What is the alternative when you experience injustice or offenses? Talk it out with God. "Lord, that really hurt.

It felt unjust. But I give it to You. You said for my former shame, pain, and disgrace there would be double recompense. I ask You for that. Give me favor in the places where I've suffered. I choose to silence the enemy in my own heart and mind and refuse the temptation to enter into judgment. I choose instead the peace Your Spirit offers me, and I look forward to experiencing Your blessing."

Being set free from judgment and unforgiveness

At one time I had issues in my relationship with my daughter when she was away from the Lord. I had started to inwardly judge the behaviors I was seeing that I didn't like. Outwardly I would smile and try to say the right things, but on many occasions she would say to me, "Stop thinking that!" People can always sense when you are judging them, and it causes them to put up walls to defend themselves against your judgments, hindering the possibility of personal connection.

One day the Holy Spirit said to me, "Your thoughts are defining her."

I said, "What do you mean, Lord?" Gently He started to explain that I was representing God to her, and what I thought about her had to line up with His feelings about her. No, He doesn't like sin. But God wanted me to realize that when He looked at her, He saw her the way He created her to be and loved her deeply, just as she was. In order to help her come from the place where she was into the place He was calling her, I needed to rid my mind of any judgments against her. So I did. I began to shift my focus from the behaviors I didn't like and instead deliberately imagined her worshipping God, pursuing Him, and loving Him. I began to see her and picture her as someone who had the motives of Christ, demonstrating the fruit of the Spirit, and started to speak to her as someone who was already saved. Her response to me was remarkable; defensive comments turned into freedom as she started embracing the love she found in my heart toward her. Little by little she started to feel safe rather than judged. Little by little I learned to see her as she was called to be and love her deeply as she was.

Now the relationship we have is sweet, and she comes to church weekly and sometimes travels with me when I minister. One week we were invited to our first mother-daughter conference where we were both invited to speak. Throughout this process the Holy Spirit was guiding and leading us both to put down the walls of judgment and defense and walk in His freedom, forgiveness, and love.

This kind of thinking is not normal for our culture in this fallen world, but it is absolutely normal in the kingdom of God. This is what Christianity should look like. I don't cover up the pain, but I have learned how to deal with it and heal from it. "Ow, that hurt! But thank You, Lord, for restoration and the promise of double recompense! Praise the Lord; it's going to work out for good!" People may think you're crazy, but you are rooting yourself in reality when you think like that. In any situation in life, you can walk in faith and hope, trusting in God's goodness. There is no need to manipulate God—give Him your most pitiful look and hope He has sympathy for you, strategize about getting even with whoever hurt you, or anything else. These are all walls we build in order to protect ourselves, but the Holy Spirit wants to help us walk free. The Holy Spirit wants to train you to walk in divine joy, righteousness, and peace. This is a life worth having, and you can have it only by letting the Spirit train you in it. It doesn't just happen. You were created with free will, and it didn't disappear when you gave your life to Christ. You still have a choice every moment of every day to follow your own will or align with God's. You can think the way the world does, or you can reckon yourself dead and think in sync with the Holy Spirit. He wants you to set your mind on things above.

When you're going through one of these mental battles, one of the most effective ways to win is to pick up the Word and begin to speak it. Declare it out loud. Ask the Holy Spirit to help you find something in Scripture to declare for that situation, and then open up with it. Declare that God makes all things work together for your good because that's what He promised to do (Rom. 8:28). Declare that He opens doors "no one can shut" (Rev. 3:8). Acknowledge that if He is for you, no one can be against you (Rom. 8:31). All these declarations are biblical promises that you can use at any time because they are always true. They are weapons of warfare to pull down strongholds and thoughts that exalt themselves against God's truth. Use them.

Be healthy and whole, both body and soul

I love to see miracles. I love to hear the testimonies of those who are healed in our meetings. I love hearing the reports that medical tests have shown that leukemia, hepatitis, diabetes, and many other diseases have left people's bodies after prayer. I love it when our people go out to pray for the sick and minister in God's power for life and healing. I believe this is how the glory of the Lord will cover the earth as the waters cover the sea. We are in a season in which His work in believers is going to go from glory to glory and strength to strength. God is going to minister to you in dreams, and you'll move in higher and higher levels of His gifting. His gifts are being poured out so His name will be lifted up. It's an exciting moment in history.

But in the midst of all that the Holy Spirit wants you to be healthy and happy and whole—body, soul, and spirit. He wants you to walk in supernatural peace that is not dependent in any way on how you're feeling at the moment or what circumstances have come against you but rather on your ability to fix your mind on God. There's a difference between knowing His truth and letting it saturate your mind. This is one of the Holy Spirit's primary areas of focus in your life because He doesn't just want to restore lives through you; He wants yours to be one of the lives restored.

In fact, these things are vitally connected. Holiness, humility, forgiveness, and power are all connected. A happy and whole believer is much more equipped to walk in the supernatural than a burdened and bitter one is. Allowing the Holy Spirit to help us continually walk free from sin is necessary if we want to experience the fullness of the power we are called to walk in.

When Jesus went to speak at the synagogue in His hometown of Nazareth, He quoted a messianic passage in Isaiah 61 and said, "Today this Scripture is fulfilled in your hearing" (Luke 4:21). They got really upset with Him and tried to throw Him off a cliff, in fact. If you look at the original passage that Jesus quoted from, it's really encouraging. The exciting thing is that in your being a joint heir with Jesus all Scriptures that are promises for Him are also promises for you. Along with Him, you get to inherit whatever He has been promised. The Isaiah 61 passage is one of my favorites, and I love to personalize it when I pray:

> The Spirit of the Sovereign LORD is upon me, for the LORD has anointed me to bring good news to the poor. He has sent me to comfort the brokenhearted and to proclaim that captives will be released and prisoners will be freed. He has sent me to tell those who mourn that the time of the LORD's favor has come, and with it, the day of God's anger against their enemies. To all who mourn in Israel, he will give a crown of beauty for ashes, a joyous blessing instead of mourning, festive praise instead of despair. In their righteousness, they will be like great oaks that the LORD has planted for his own glory.
> —ISAIAH 61:1–3, NLT

Beauty instead of ashes. Life instead of death. Righteousness instead of unrighteousness, the nature of God in place of iniquity, praise instead of despair—these are amazing promises! We get the mind of Christ instead of confusion, delight over a downcast heart, and supernatural hope instead of depression. In so many ways this passage promises the answers to our deepest problems.

That's all very exciting, but you will not be able to experience these things unless you allow them to become more than concepts with which you agree. The Holy Spirit wants to help you meditate on these truths until they are spiritually digested and have become your deep inner conviction. No matter how much Scripture you are able to quote, it is still possible to walk in torment and unbelief. If you take the simplicity of the gospel and God's promises at face value, meditating on them and applying them, they will impact your heart and change you. You will be able to put aside judgment and thank God you don't have to carry that burden anymore. You can cast off worries and trust God to carry them Himself. God wants to give you life instead of death, but much of what goes in our minds brings death if we give the thoughts room. That's what Scripture says: the mind set on the flesh is death (Rom. 8:6). Thinking in the world's ways will kill you. But if your mind is submitted to the Holy Spirit—if you take captive the thoughts that come against you and say, "No, I'm not going there"—you will walk in peace. As you choose life-giving thoughts, you will experience abundant life. Take up the sword of the Spirit and declare the truth, and the truth will make you free (John 8:32). You don't need to strive for joy; you can just live in it by faith. It's your inheritance.

Chapter 8

THE HOLY SPIRIT AND VICTORY

T HE HOLY SPIRIT is longing to move through us, His followers, in ways beyond what we have even imag ined. We're about to see the gifts of the Spirit revealed in greater ways and measure than we have yet seen, and that will be astonishing. People will not know exactly how to respond. God will glorify Himself in a powerful way through His bride. Right now the bride is making herself ready, and the Holy Spirit is supernaturally stirring us and enlightening our hearts, awakening us to know the power of walking in His victory.

Preparing for Victory

Part of our preparation for victory is valuing the Word of God by reading and praying the Bible. I made a CD of myself praying biblical prayers and promises set to worship music (*Prayers of His People*) because I believe it's extremely important to develop the habit of praying and declaring the Word of God and making it personal. It is a key to living in victory. Something powerful happens when we fellowship with the Holy Spirit and the Word, declare His promises, and come into agreement with what the Holy Spirit is doing. When we declare what His Word says with heartfelt gratitude and faith, things change. Confessing the Word of God in faith and fellowshipping with the Holy Spirit are operating in the image of the One who created the world with His words. God says we can have whatever we ask for according to His will, and we can be confident that whatever we pray for from His Word is His will (1 John 5:14–15). We pray not from an attitude of hoping it might happen but from a confidence that He will do what He said. As we attach faith to our requests, the Holy Spirit leads us into victory.

Isaiah 62:10 tells us to "build up the highway" and cast out the stones. So as we fellowship with the Holy Spirit, if we feel Him showing us issues that need to be surrendered, we can cast them away through prayer and experience a divine acceleration into victory. This is a season for traveling fast. That's what highways are for. The heart of the Holy Spirit is for us to take out everything that would slow us down or cause us to stumble so we can fly with Him and manifest His glory. As we recognize anything in our lives that doesn't line up with the revelation of who God is, we need to be willing to yield it up. As we discipline ourselves by responding to the Holy Spirit, training our senses in discerning right from wrong, our ability to have influence and acceleration increases. God's ways are higher and better than our ways (Isa. 55:9), and the Holy Spirit is with us to teach us to walk in Christ, who is "the way, the truth, and the life" (John 14:6). He equips and empowers us to be overcomers.

Overcoming Obstacles Through Faith

I realize that Scripture tells us we will have trouble in this world. There's no getting around that. But Jesus has already overcome the world, so in Him we are overcomers (John 16:33). He gives us everything we need pertaining to "life and godliness" (2 Pet. 1:3). It's already ours. We have to wake up and actually use it, but we don't have to strive to attain it. So when trials come, there's no reason to have a pity party about them, saying, "Poor me; I'm under attack." No, it's normal. If you weren't under attack and dealing with warfare, you might not be human. The enemy hates everyone made in the image of God and seeks to destroy them. So trials are normal. But for us so is overcoming them. We already have everything we need to walk in the victory won for us in Christ.

If the Holy Spirit is preparing a platform for His people, and if it is in His nature to overcome obstacles and trials, then doesn't it make sense that those who partner with Him will find that they overcome in Him? While many believers are asking the Holy Spirit to do something for them, He is asking us to "live and move and have our being" in Him (Acts 17:28). He is the One who overcomes. In Him so do we.

I've heard people say they don't want to get too on fire for God because they're afraid of the warfare that will come as a result. That doesn't make much sense to me. It's our intimacy with the Holy Spirit that causes us to be victorious. Some people run away from God to avoid opposition, and that's not a very safe place at all. The enemy comes and tramples on them. You are going to have warfare either way, but would you rather be close to Him in a place of overcoming or on the fringes of the flock in a place of vulnerability? Drawing close to God increases the power that flows through you. You have confidence there that others don't have. You are not a victim there. Yes, be sober and alert. Vigilance is vital. But fear is absolutely unnecessary. You are in a victorious position already.

God has not called us to live casually or passively. There is an old song titled "Que Sera Sera" that says whatever is going to happen will happen. This is not a good motto for a believer. I want to live deliberately in the Spirit, recognizing that I've been given a set number of days to steward well. I want to take captive every thought that exalts itself against the knowledge of Christ so my mind can be controlled by the Holy Spirit, and I can walk with power. That mind-set is life and peace. That means exercising our free will continuously to choose Him as Lord. He's in charge. We don't have to struggle with anxiety because we've cast our cares on Him, and He is trustworthy to carry them. We don't have to be caught up in fear because His promises over us are certain. We can just lean back into Him as John did at the Last Supper (John 13:23). We yield to Him and thank Him for empowering us. When we remind ourselves that "it is no longer [we] who live, but Christ who lives in [us]" (Gal. 2:20), we begin to experience the power of that reality. We don't have to work to put our carnal natures to death; we will forever be frustrated if we keep trying to die because that's still focusing on ourselves. How can we put the flesh to death in the power of the flesh? We can't. We can reckon ourselves dead to self and alive to Christ only by the power of the Holy Spirit (Rom. 6:11). We receive the reality of our crucifixion and resurrection with Jesus by grace through faith. It's a gift. He's alive in us. We are to live intentionally and deliberately in His life and not our own because His victory is ours.

If you're worried you don't have enough faith for that, ask the Holy Spirit to help you access your gift of faith! Faith is a gift you have already been given; you don't need to go out and get it. You need to let it rise up within you through fellowship with the Holy Spirit. Instead of striving for it, thank Him for it. It will grow the more you consider that it is already there. He says you have the mind of Christ, so you do. Don't strive for it; live from it by faith with the Holy Spirit's help. You have the motives and desires of Christ. Anytime the enemy tries to clutter your mind with something else, take up the sword of the Spirit, and recognize those thoughts as intruders and evict them. No one sits there twiddling his thumbs when an intruder invades his home, right? In the Holy Spirit live with the same level of vigilance, and experience the victory you have already been given.

This is how we overcome:

> If with heart and soul you're doing good, do you think you can be stopped? Even if you suffer for it, you're still better off. Don't give the opposition a second thought. Through thick and thin, keep your hearts at attention, in adoration before Christ, your Master. Be ready to speak up and tell anyone who asks why you're living the way you are, and always with the utmost courtesy. Keep a clear conscience before God so that when people throw mud at you,

none of it will stick. They'll end up realizing that *they're* the ones who need a bath. It's better to suffer for doing good, if that's what God wants, than to be punished for doing bad.

—1 PETER 3:13–17, THE MESSAGE

"Through thick and thin, keep your hearts at attention, in adoration before Christ." That's what we've been talking about, isn't it? When someone comes hurling accusations or doing hurtful things, instead of focusing on the offenses and getting into judgments, don't even give it a second thought. The opposition is not worthy of your attention. Jesus is. Through thick and thin, keep your eyes and your adoration on Him. A heart focused on Him is a heart that overcomes.

The Holy Spirit longs for us to walk in the simplicity of devotion to Christ—loving and worshipping Him, with minds given over to Him and fixed on things above. If you preoccupy yourself with why people are insensitive and self-centered—and though that feels instinctual, it is a habit you've developed and can choose to change—you have been distracted from what is pure and lovely and of a good report. You've actually begun to partner with the pain that torments you. Cut that partnership off, engage with the Holy Spirit, and keep your heart fixed in a place of adoration of Him. Life is a lot less complicated this way. It puts you in a position of being able to partner with the Holy Spirit to reveal His glory.

It's easy to fall into the pattern of the world. You'll have no trouble finding somebody who is selfish or jealous or overly ambitious to complain about. Whatever your justification for making those judgments, it is actually an attempt to elevate yourself by cutting others down. But even if that helps you feel better for a moment, in the long run it creates a problem. It continually exacerbates the pain you feel, and every time you think about that person, the judgment returns, and you limit your capacity to love. You remain a victim, hindering yourself from accessing the victory already won for you.

Walking in the Simplicity of Faith

The Holy Spirit wants to help us walk in victory by living in the faith of Jesus. Many people know in their minds that God is a good Father, but they have trouble expecting Him to be good to them personally. They have no trouble believing He will be good to others, but doubts block them from believing He will bring victory in their specific situations. So they come up with all sorts of complex reasons why God doesn't intervene in this or that situation, or explain delays and contradictions in their lives that may or may not fit with His true nature. But God's nature does not change from person to person or time to time; He does not play favorites (Acts 10:34), and He does not change (Mal. 3:6; Heb. 13:8). That is why Jesus pointed again and again to the faith of children as an example (Matt. 18:4; 19:14), which we will explore a bit more in chapter 11. The Holy Spirit will always bring us back to the simplicity of faith. He will bring you back to the truth that He alone has the words of life. He fills us with the faith of a child and then responds to that kind of faith to bring us into victory.

This is the kind of faith that overcomes obstacles and opposition in our lives because it perseveres through them.

A child says, "This is what my father said," and it is very hard to persuade him otherwise because he knows what his father is like. Jesus said, "Whoever says to this mountain, 'Be removed and be thrown into the sea,' and does not doubt in his heart, but believes that what he says will come to pass, he will have whatever he says. Therefore I say to you, whatever things you ask when you pray, believe that you will receive them, and you will have them" (Mark 11:23–24). The Holy Spirit does not complicate things for us. He inspires and honors this kind of faith. He wants us to believe simply, and simply believe.

We see this convergence of pure love and simple faith often in the New Testament. Paul writes, "Now the goal of this command is love from a pure heart, and from a good conscience, and from sincere faith. From this, some have lost their way and turned aside to empty talk" (1 Tim. 1:5–6). God's desire for us is always to come back to the simplicity of walking with a pure heart, a clean conscience, and a sincere faith. In order to do that, we have to stop giving a second thought—or third, fourth, or fifth thought—to the things we've suffered at the hands of others or to the obstacles that are in our way. Instead take them to the Lord.

I've had to learn to release and persevere through pain—to practice simple faith—because sometimes the weight becomes so heavy I can't cope. Scripture tells us we can take all the pain, shame, and dishonor we've experienced and sow it in faith to receive double blessing (Isa. 61:7; Zech. 9:12). "Thank You for the double recompense You are going to bring." He is faithful, even when our pain is our own fault, to restore us and bless us doubly for the trouble we've endured if we will sow our pain into the soil of His kingdom in faith. This is our victory in Him.

I am thankful I have incredible favor on the Internet and in the media, but there have been times when I didn't. Someone who never met me and doesn't know me made a video because the person was angry that I am a woman who preaches the gospel. Without having ever met me or been to one of my meetings, this person decided to go online to warn others about me. There is nothing I can do to change the fact that God created me female.

I was watching this video one day, and Tom told me not to. "Stop it. Turn it off," he said. It hadn't occurred to me that I could just ignore it, but that's what Tom told me to do. I never even saw the whole thing.

Tom was right. Why was I even listening to that? It wasn't pure, lovely, or of good report. So instead of wallowing in the pain of that, we deliberately released the pain and said, "Lord, we sow this dishonor on the Internet for double. We ask for double honor and favor online and on the airways according to Your promise." And God's returns are amazing! Google me now, and you'll see incredible favor. There's nothing the enemy can throw at you that you can't sow back and get a glorious return. Jesus assured His followers they could rejoice over their persecution and insults. He warned us that not everyone would speak well of us, but there's no reason to absorb the pain of these things and harbor bitterness and resentment. Release the pain, and have faith that God will honor His promises and your childlike faith, and victory over obstacles will come.

The Holy Spirit is so wonderful when it comes to

comforting us. He knows our pain and can interpret our tears. He wants to show you that your pain and judgments will never get someone else to repent. They reduce your capacity to love. But if you let them go, you release yourself from continual torment and set yourself up for blessing. You move from being a victim to being an overcomer—to being victorious.

Come back to the simplicity of the gospel. The Holy Spirit is leading you there because that's the place where He can fill you with love and power. Let Him build up your faith, patience, and perseverance. As Paul writes, "Overcome evil with good" (Rom. 12:21). Overflow with the love and wisdom of the Spirit in every situation. You can walk in victory and peace. You can radiate with the glory of God. You are being set up as a platform for the amazing work God is doing in this world. The Holy Spirit is partnering with you to make you a display of God's goodness. Your freedom, your peace, and your overcoming love will transform lives.

Chapter 9

THE SPIRIT OF
SUPERNATURAL PEACE

W E LIVE IN a restless world. People read the headlines and are full of fear and anxiety. They look for security and can't find it in any other human being, any position or accomplishment, or any set of circumstances. The deep longing of their hearts is for peace—the *shalom* of God's kingdom that we were designed to experience. They want their hearts to be at rest.

When we walk in turmoil and restlessness, we cannot have the power with which the Holy Spirit wants to fill our lives. He has to do an inner work in us in order for us to bear outward fruit. He has to change the way we think. That doesn't mean we have to qualify for His favor or spend years in a never-ending process before we can do the works of God. I've seen new believers do miraculous works on day one, but if we want to walk in the Spirit as a lifestyle, our internal environment needs to change. We need supernatural peace.

The Cry for More

I love to pray the Bible. I made my CD of the apostolic prayers in Scripture because I know there is tremendous power in praying God's Word. The Bible tells us we can have whatever we pray according to His will, so when we read His will in His Word, we can know our prayers that line up with that will be answered. We can pray, declare, believe, and then receive it. When we pray and believe who He is and that He has made us righteous through His Son, we can have the boldness to ask whatever we will. The Holy Spirit wants to give you supernatural peace that He is faithful and trustworthy. The amazing promises of God and tremendous peace are available to anyone who will ask in faith.

When God started to give me favor and promotion with the media, my heart cried, "Oh, God, help me." It was a little overwhelming. But I felt the Holy Spirit quicken me to begin to pray from Revelation 3:14–22, that God would give me eye salve to see so I wouldn't think I was rich and full and in need of nothing. I needed the grace to recognize continually my deep need and longing for Him. Only God can provide what I most need, and it all flows from my fellowship with Him. He doesn't want to be a Band-Aid that helps us every now and then when we need a fix. He wants to be our life source, integrally involved in every aspect of our lives. So I prayed for supernatural sight to see and continually recognize my need for the Holy Spirit.

It is His delight and desire to be there for us in every circumstance of life and for us to live in peace as a result of knowing this. I believe that during this time, a time when so many are seeking the Lord and asking for eye salve to see Him more clearly, He has been fine-tuning our hearts. It's no coincidence that He has been doing this in His church all over the world. I believe He is preparing us for the greatest outpouring of glory the world has ever seen.

Many are crying out for more. I want more too—to see more than I've seen, know Him better than I've known Him, and love Him more than I've loved Him. We're not content to have church as normal, and that's good. But we already have everything we need. He has already given us all of Himself. He didn't give us just a portion of the Spirit; He gave us the Spirit. The cry for more is deep calling out to deep, a longing to experience more and have greater awareness. But this is more a matter of stepping into what we already have, not receiving something new. It's growing in our knowledge of what He has given and what we can freely access in Him.

I believe the Holy Spirit has been conditioning our minds to understand this and bringing us to a place where our hearts are so uncluttered that we can be truly filled with all His peace and fullness, just as He promised. We are in a tremendous season of awakening and revival, and the Spirit wants us to recognize His power right now, yield to Him, and let Him take us into deeper and deeper levels.

I've shared about how easy it is for our minds to embrace judgments we were not made to carry. This robs us of the peace God intends for us to have. The kingdom of God is righteousness, peace, and joy, not heaviness and judgment. I received a testimony recently from a lady at church who had not realized how much judgment she had placed on the people who had hurt her. Similar to many believers she had released forgiveness to people again and again but then kept remembering her pain and being tormented by it. This lady went home after the service where I had been sharing about this and spent hours asking the Spirit to remind her of the scenes she had been playing in her head. She asked God to forgive her for judging each person she had judged and finally felt released from the pain of those situations. She got to a place of thinking of those people without feeling pain anymore. That's such a precious testimony and also an example of what God is doing among us. He wants us to be able to walk in supernatural peace with our eyes fixed on Him and what He wants to do through us.

This is what the cry for more can bring us to. The Spirit knows how to help us as His Word does surgery in our hearts. Don't ever become so fascinated with what God is doing that you forget you need His Word in your heart and life as a plumb line. One passage I've found helpful lately is from Luke 21. Jesus said, "Take heed to yourselves, lest your hearts become burdened by excessiveness and drunkenness and anxieties of life, and that Day comes on you unexpectedly" (v. 34). It's fascinating to me that Jesus mentions drunkenness and the anxieties of life in the same breath. People who are drunk don't see clearly. They become disoriented. In a lot of ways the anxieties of life do exactly the same thing to us. They distort our vision and prevent us from seeing clearly and walking straight. Those judgments and worries that torment us clutter our hearts and disorient us so we don't have an accurate perception of reality. We get consumed with trying to figure out what's going on and why it happened, and the Holy Spirit wants us to be very careful about that. It's as dangerous as wasting your life in a state of drunkenness. It will keep you from anticipating and experiencing His movements.

Peace That Surpasses Understanding

I believe prophetically that it is of vital importance for us to embrace the Prince of Peace right now. The Bible says that the mind controlled by the Spirit "is life and peace" (Rom. 8:6). Even though we will have troubles in the world, Jesus has "overcome the world" (John 16:33). The Spirit wants to be our practical help in this. We have to embrace the revelation of peace in a world that is filled with fear and turmoil—what many would say is the opposite of peace. You won't get this by reading the headlines every day; there's not a lot of peace in the world. But the peace of God surpasses understanding (Phil. 4:7). We get it from being rooted in another realm. It has been given to us as a gift not only so we will have a happy life but also so we will have a powerful weapon that helps us live with clarity of vision.

Some friends of ours recently had their first baby. Nathaniel works on staff with us, and he and his wife, Hayley, were very excited for their little girl to arrive. Gabriella was born on a Saturday morning. Hayley had asked the Lord to give her a supernatural peace throughout the whole birthing process, and Gabriella was born without any complications. They called to let me know the good news soon after she was born early that morning. I was on my way to speak at a conference a little later that day when I received a call from the hospital. The midwife sounded quite concerned, and she asked me to come quickly to the hospital. The baby had experienced a heart attack, and her heart had stopped for four minutes before they had been able to resuscitate her. Gabriella's condition was rapidly deteriorating, and the nursing staff had suggested that a support person be called.

As I walked into the hospital's intensive care unit, the nurses met me and asked if I was the minister. They quickly filled me in and explained that it seemed as though Nathaniel and Hayley didn't understand how serious the situation was. I think they were hoping I would help prepare Nathaniel and Hayley for the worst. I remember thinking to myself, "You have the wrong person."

As I walked in and saw Gabriella on life support, my first response was, "Let's take a photo. This is going to be a wonderful testimony."

That is how the supernatural peace of the Holy Spirit operates in our lives; He releases peace that passes understanding (Phil. 4:7). We prayed and thanked God for His healing power and promises. I asked the nurses to help Hayley start expressing milk because this baby would be feeding soon, and we wanted to keep up Hayley's milk supply. They looked at me and seemed rather puzzled but did as I asked.

Gabriella was transferred to another hospital and for the next two days was completely unresponsive. We had the church pray, and a prophetic word was given that on the third day, Gabriella would rise again. As I went in to see them each day, the peace of the Holy Spirit continued to keep Nathaniel and Hayley in faith even though Gabriella's lungs had collapsed, and she continued to deteriorate. The peace of the Holy Spirit is a powerful weapon because it refuses to give place to fear. Early one morning the doctor tried to help Nathaniel come to terms with the fact that it was highly likely Gabriella had suffered severe brain damage from being without oxygen for so long. Medically speaking that was the most likely reason they had seen no response from her. Nathaniel looked at the doctor and asked him what he would need to see in order to have hope that she would survive. The doctor said she would need to at least open her eyes and that he would be astonished if they even saw that. Nathaniel's response was, "Get ready to be astonished because I know God will heal her." Nathaniel then went into another room by himself and deliberately laid hold of the peace he knew the Holy Spirit wanted him to maintain.

The next morning, on the third day, Gabriella opened her eyes. And from that moment on she was healed. The doctors could find nothing wrong with her. To everyone's amazement she was breathing on her own and was completely healthy.[1]

The Holy Spirit wants us to live with a heavenly mindset so we can release His peace on earth. That's why Jesus was excited to go away; the Holy Spirit is an incredible gift who will bless the world through us. We need to be ambassadors of peace—not just the absence of conflict that the world is striving for but the supernatural ability to live with an uncluttered heart. The outpouring is coming to deliver people from torment, and it can come only through people who have been freed from it and live in the supernatural peace of the Holy Spirit.

As you enter into a new way of thinking and partner with the Holy Spirit to renew your mind, your capacity to carry His glory will increase dramatically. As you give no place to the whys and the temptations of the enemy to clutter your heart with anxieties and judgments, you will have increasing ability to hear the heartbeat of the Father and the sounds of heaven. The more you lean into the Holy Spirit's arms, the more you will recognize the plans God has for the world. God has a greater plan for your life than just to be a church member or a believer who settles for the status quo. He has a greater plan than having you win a few people here and there to Jesus, as great as that is. His plan is that you would be revealed as a gift on the earth through the power of the Holy Spirit—a manifestation of the children of God that all creation is waiting for and eagerly expecting (Rom. 8:19). He wants you to recognize that because you carry the Prince of Peace within you, you carry the power to transform the world. The heart of the Holy Spirit is for you to realize what you have, know the hope of your calling, and understand your value to Him and to the world. God is very excited about your life. He doesn't want you to get preoccupied with things that will cause you to strive for nothing more than survival and coping. He has laid up good works in advance for you to do (Eph. 2:10), and they are astounding.

Sometimes people talk about the "normal" Christian life, and the definition of that may differ from person to person. But I believe we're stepping into a new understanding of what normal is. What would it be like if all believers walked in supernatural peace? How much would God do through us if every time we met someone, we no longer tried to get some sort of affirmation from that person or no longer felt compelled to talk to them about our problems but walked into situations knowing we already have the answer inside us? Too many Christians and ministers are wondering, "Do I have a ministry? Am I good enough?" The truth is that we have the Son of God in us, and we can walk not in arrogance about that but in absolute confidence that we have the desire of nations in us and on us. Divine peace is a powerful testimony.

Carriers of Glory

If we live as though we have nothing to prove and believe we carry the glory of God within us, we will be genuinely excited for everyone we meet. We will wake up in the morning anticipating that everyone we meet will be blessed through encountering the Holy Spirit in us. Without any arrogance at all we will expect people to have a divine encounter when they meet us because we radiate who He is.

This takes more than theological knowledge. It requires an experiential response to Jesus. Knowledge puffs up, but an encounter transforms us. Some people have knowledge but walk around as though they are God's gift to the world because of their own talents and expertise. That's not what

I'm talking about. Those who say, "I've been crucified with Jesus and have been forgiven; He now lives in me, and I get to overflow with His love for everyone else," will begin to experience transforming power.

The world is waiting for that. The nations are opening to us. God has been up to something, opening the doors of nations to the revelation of His Son through the power of His Holy Spirit. I see it in Australia, and I also see it in the countries I've visited. I believe we are being given a divine opportunity to bring the reality of who Christ is as the Prince of Peace into our society. People are longing for Him, even when they don't know that's what they are longing for. As His beautiful bride begins to awaken and recognize who He is and who we are, nations will be blessed.

We have suffered unnecessarily for too long under false burdens. I can be ridiculously sensitive when someone hurts me, and it takes time to get over it. I'm not very good at saying, "Who cares?" I actually care, even when I'm not supposed to, but the Holy Spirit wants us to see the trap in the things that weigh us down. They are all designed to steal our focus, to distract us from our higher purpose. They clutter up our minds, make our hearts feel heavy, and cause us to miss out on the full picture of what He wants to do.

Think of the contrast. What is it like to interact with someone who is radiating joy and supernatural peace, even when he or she is dealing with difficult things in life? When Stephen was being arrested and stoned (recorded in Acts 6 and 7), his face shone like that of an angel. He wasn't saying, "This is so unfair! I haven't done anything wrong!" He wasn't despondent about this sudden turn of events. He glowed with the glory of God. He saw Jesus standing at the right hand of the Father. His attitude made no sense to the people who were persecuting him, but it became a testimony for others. It was supernatural.

That's what is available to you and me. It's what people will remember from their interactions with us. They may not remember the words we say or the things we do, but they will remember the attitude we carry. Radiance makes a lasting impression. Let people be as nasty as they want. If you determine in your heart not to get into judgment, you will shine with glory and peace, and people will notice. You were created with hinds' feet to walk in high places. You were designed for divine peace. You have the authority to pick up the sword of the Spirit and say "peace" to storms. It is not your purpose in life to be a victim or to be overcome; your purpose is to be an overcomer. Worship and battle with the supernatural gifts of the Holy Spirit you've been given, and shine with the radiance of God.

Peace That Changes the World

One of the reasons John Wesley, a theologian, was converted was because he saw supernatural peace in the lives of the Moravians. He was traveling from England to Georgia, and a fierce storm threatened the ship. The decks were flooded, and the sails were torn. Most of the passengers were terrified, but a group of Moravian missionaries sang hymns and worshipped without any fear of death. Wesley was a preacher, but he didn't have what they had. Their peace made such an impression on him that he wrote about it in his journal and hung on to the memory throughout his time in Georgia, which did not go well. When he was back in England two years later someone invited him to a Moravian prayer meeting. He went and was converted that night.[2]

The Spirit wants us to walk in that kind of peace no matter what is going on around us. He wants our peace to confound people. Just as Jesus spoke to the storm to "be still" (Mark 4:39), the Spirit wants us to be so at rest in Him that the storms outside of us have to bow to the peace inside of us. When we are saturated in light, the enemy has to run. Our peace can change the world.

The moment light exposes deception, deceptive forces have no chance. That applies to demonic oppression and to any other form of darkness. The moment you see what is happening—when you are in a situation in which you feel stressed or weighed down—the darkness begins to flee. In the natural your feelings may be entirely justified. But you don't walk according to the natural. You are not a mere human. If you have been born again, you have been called to something higher. You are no longer subject to these things.

I had a lovely dream recently. I had been feeling a little stressed, but the Lord was there in my dream. We were walking and talking, and Jesus was right in the midst of a situation I was concerned about. The peace that came with His presence made the situation seem powerless to hurt me. I had nothing to be worried about. No one needs to be worried about anything when Jesus is there, right? It was as though His presence meant that the usual rules didn't apply. It was similar to the feeling you used to get when your parents would come to school in the middle of the day to take you home for a special occasion. Their presence meant that suddenly a higher authority had come in, and the rules you were normally subject to didn't apply. You were free to go home when others were not. The presence of the Holy Spirit means we can walk above the worries of the world. I woke up feeling such wonderful peace in my heart. I thought, "What on earth was I worried about?" My stress seemed so irrelevant.

What happened in my dream is true in reality all the time. The Holy Spirit is always with us. The normal rules don't apply. The Holy Spirit wants to open the eyes to His peace that passes understanding. The more we grow to understand Him and know His presence, the more we realize that the normal patterns that used to govern our minds no longer apply. The rules have changed. We get to walk in supernatural peace now. We are no longer victims. We are seated in heavenly places, ruling and reigning with Him.

Chapter 10

THE SPIRIT OF INTERCESSION

G OD'S WORD IS alive. It is rich, powerful, glorious truth, and He wants to speak to you personally through His Word to refresh and encourage you. He doesn't want you just to know what He is saying to you; He wants you to *know* it deep down in your spirit, the kind of knowing that is unquestionable and unshakeable. There are times when you are walking through a situation and don't know which way to go; you may not even know how to pray. God will quicken things from His Word and bring them to mind, but sometimes it still isn't clear. The Word tells you to stand still and see the salvation of God, and it also tells you to move forward in faith, and sometimes your memory will bring both to mind (Exod. 14:13). Both are biblical, but you don't know which one to choose for the moment. The Holy Spirit wants to help in times such as these to guide and instruct. But He does even more than that—He helps you pray.

Romans 8:26 begins, "The Spirit helps us in our weaknesses"—not just in prayer but in everything. That means whenever you feel as if you're floundering and not

151

coping well, you can cry out, and He is there to help. The verse continues, "…we do not know what to pray for as we ought, but the Spirit Himself intercedes for us with groanings too deep for words." I don't know everything I need to pray about. Sometimes I'm completely unaware of a situation, and other times I know I need to be praying about an issue but don't understand what is really happening. But the Holy Spirit knows everything—in this realm and in the spirit realm. He knows every detail of the circumstances and every corner of people's hearts. It would be impossible for you to cover all the essential details of a situation in your own words in prayer, but He will pray through you as you partner with Him and open your mouth. And His prayers are always effective.

Your victories and triumphs are directly linked to your partnering with the Holy Spirit in prayer. Exodus 17 tells the story of Joshua's battle against the Amalekites, and as long as Moses was interceding with his hands raised, Joshua's army prevailed. But when Moses let down his hands, the enemy got the advantage. Our prayers are like that with the Holy Spirit as our partner in intercession. Effective prayer is not an accident. We prevail when we rely on the power of His prayers through us. The Lord is very intentional about teaching us that we are not earthly beings anymore. We are supernatural, new creations in Christ who are seated in heavenly places. There's no reason for us to try to do the works of God as mere humans. Prayer connects us with God's overcoming power. Praying in the Spirit is a supernatural experience. That's why we can minister to people in our own strength and see nothing happen, but when we lean back into the Holy Spirit and let Him work, prayers and prophetic words immediately begin to accomplish things.

The Holy Spirit is aware of exactly what you need, even the things you don't know you need. He sets up divine appointments, arranges circumstances, repairs broken walls, restores lost blessings, provides unexpected opportunities, and fills your life with His kindness. When we really begin to grasp that, prayer doesn't seem like a chore at all. It goes from being a distraction to being the main event. We jump at the opportunity because we know what prayer in the Spirit accomplishes.

Spirit-Led Intercession

Spirit-led prayer can take many different forms. It might be silent and subdued at times and rather loud and intense at others. Hebrews 5:7 tells us that Jesus "offered up prayers and supplications with loud cries and tears." Sometimes prayer might consist of a brief request, and sometimes it may be a long, drawn-out process. It may seem effortless or heavy. Paul wrote to the Colossians that Epaphras was "always laboring fervently" for them in his prayers (Col. 4:12), and the word he used implied an intense wrestling—the same word we get *agonize* from. The Holy Spirit may inspire prayer in your own language, another human language, or a heavenly language. In other words, He fills your spirit and your mouth with many kinds of prayers that manifest in all sorts of ways.

I believe the heart of intercession is simply being a friend of God. The eyes of the Lord are looking throughout the earth for those whose hearts are His and are available to come into agreement with Him (2 Chron. 16:9). Because He has given us the keys of the kingdom, we have to come into agreement with the plans of heaven to see His will done on earth. The Holy Spirit will move us to pray and show us how, often giving us scripture as a launching point. I love to pray the Bible. You can always begin there, but sometimes you will also find that He puts someone or a specific situation on your heart.

I remember that as a young mother I would often be trying to put the baby to sleep and have someone on my mind. Later I would see this person at church and say, "I had you on my mind this week."

"Oh, were you praying for me?" she would ask.

Well, no, I hadn't been. But after so many times I began to realize that this was an invitation for intercession, and I would begin to lift people up whenever they came into my thoughts. After a while I sensed the Holy Spirit leading me in these prayers, and then bit by bit He would give me visions and words of knowledge about situations. If you are faithful with what He gives you and respond to His invitations, intercession becomes a wonderful adventure with Him. As you prove trustworthy, He shares His secrets with you. It's a delight.

You can't be a prophet and not be an intercessor. If you get words from Him, you almost always find an invitation to pray somewhere in them. The prophetic gifts and intercession go together very powerfully when covered in love. Love will not always lead you to say the thing you're hearing from the Lord; sometimes you know you've heard only so you can pray. The point is to see the Word of God accomplished, and intercession is vital to that process. Our hearts and minds have to be free to love, to hear the Father, and to respond to what He says. Intercession is often the very thing that we are to occupy ourselves with in place of the worries and judgments we used to carry.

There have been times when I was driving and had to pull over to the side of the road because the Spirit moved me to pray. I would turn off the car and begin to pray as the Holy Spirit led me and showed me things that were going on. I'd groan, cry, and pray, and then the burden would lift. Often I would get a phone call later and find out what the Holy Spirit was doing in that moment and how He used me to partner with Him. I once felt a strong urge to pray in the middle of a dinner, and I had to excuse myself with apologies and send my guests home so I could pray. I found out later that Tom had been in a precarious situation overseas at that moment. He confirmed that the streets I had seen whilst praying in the Spirit and the danger I had sensed were exactly what he was experiencing. The Holy Spirit had answered my prayers and made a way out.

Perfect Prayers

I was about fourteen when I got baptized in the Holy Spirit. I went into a back room at church with a group of other people to pray for the baptism. "You're going to speak in new tongues," we were told. So we prayed, and I spoke in new tongues. "That's great," I thought, but I didn't know what to do with it. I would pray in the Spirit in prayer meetings because that's what others did, but I didn't know what else it was for. When I began to understand the power of praying in the Spirit—that it was the Holy Spirit praying perfect prayers through me—I began to do so much more regularly. I realized He was going before me to make my paths straight and set things up for me.

When you receive the baptism of the Holy Spirit and begin to speak in new tongues, the Spirit of God, the helper, actually prays through you, as we read in Romans 8:26. We've heard wonderful testimonies of people going through very difficult experiences in the natural realm, and when they began to pray in the Spirit, God brought a miracle. The Spirit utters perfect prayers in "groanings too deep for words," and breakthrough comes (Rom. 8:26).

In my early twenties I had just read Jackie Pullinger's book *Chasing the Dragon*. It's a great book. The author states that when she received the baptism in the Spirit, she didn't know what to do with it either. She thought, "I'll just pray 15 minutes a day." After about six weeks of doing that, she went from seeing no one getting saved to seeing people getting saved all over the place.[1] I thought I would try the same thing, so I set my timer each day and began to do what she did. I don't think I had ever prayed in tongues for more than five minutes at a time. The first time I tried this, I began to feel something happening deep in my spirit after about five minutes. My tongues began to change, my groanings became deeper, and the intercession felt stronger. After fifteen minutes I didn't want to stop, so I kept going a bit longer. Soon it became habit to pray for lengthy periods in the Spirit because I knew He was doing something powerful. Things started to shift in my life. Amazing breakthroughs started to happen. The Holy Spirit knows what is going on around me so much better than I do. He prayed prayers through me that lined up perfectly with God's will.

I'm not exactly a morning person. Sometimes when I get up and pray in the mornings, I feel as if my prayers aren't breaking through. But if I pray in the Spirit in faith, I know He knows exactly what I need and what I'm longing for. He also knows the opposition that has been sent against me, and He knows exactly how to target it in prayer. I don't have to just take a stab in the dark with my prayers. I can let Him pray through me and fight for me about the things I can't see. After a little while my thoughts become clearer as if the air has started to clear. The Spirit of Christ has been interceding for me, and that's more effective than we can understand.

One of the stories in Jackie Pullinger's book is about a man in Hong Kong who was sentenced to death by hanging. She had only a brief opportunity to share Jesus with him outside the courtroom before he was sentenced, but he prayed to accept Christ and repented of his sins, and she prayed for him to receive the baptism of the Spirit. For two years while he was on death row she was not allowed to see him. Eventually his death sentence was commuted to life imprisonment, and Jackie was allowed to go see him again. He knew little about God and had not had a Bible in those two years. All he had was his born-again and Spirit-baptism experience. She assumed he had forgotten most of what she had told him. But when she finally saw him, he was absolutely radiant. She said she had never before seen such pure joy on a man's face. He had been praying in tongues every morning and night. He didn't know what he was saying, but he believed it was a God-given language that was very powerful. He gave Jackie a list of names of other prisoners he had told about Jesus and who had been saved. He had been running a small group for them to teach them about Jesus![2]

That's the power of praying in tongues. The Holy Spirit teaches people about Jesus even when they don't have a Bible or an opportunity to be taught. He reveals what we need to know, and He prays through us in power. We are never lacking when we depend on the Holy Spirit.

When we pray in tongues, we're uttering things that are mysterious to us, and God is downloading mysteries into our spirits. He is empowering us to pray perfect prayers. I run out of words and ways to express my love sometimes when I'm worshipping. When this happens, I speak in tongues. The Holy Spirit helps us worship in spirit and in truth, giving us the language to express deep spiritual things (John 4:24).

A Diverse Gift

It's important to recognize the different sides of God's language gifts. Paul writes about praying in unknown tongues, which is what we mean when we talk about praying in the Spirit. He says that when he prays in a tongue, his spirit prays, but his "understanding is unfruitful" (1 Cor. 14:14). So, similar to Paul, we can engage our minds and ask the Holy Spirit to enlighten our understanding. He then begins to show us how to pray, and we often will get downloads of things to pray about. You can pray in the spirit and with your mind at the same time. Even if you don't understand the words you're saying, you often will understand the heart behind your prayers and have a picture of what God wants to do. Tongues are a form of worship but with words that are beyond our capacity to give God. However, we still know whom we are worshipping, and our focus is on Him. When the Spirit in us cries out, "Abba, Father," we are engaging in deep levels of worship. Tongues are a powerful part of that. It's wonderful to pray and worship in unknown tongues.

Paul also talks about the gift of tongues. This is an example of people speaking (not praying) in known languages (still unknown to the speaker but known to the hearer) for the purpose of edification. I have experienced this. Once when I was preaching, I got excited, and out came some tongues. A lady in the congregation came up to me afterward and asked if I spoke Indonesian. I don't know it, but I was praising God in Indonesian in the middle of my message. Another time I was praying in the Spirit with some ladies, and a woman from Africa told me I was praising God in her dialect. This is what happened on the Day of Pentecost when the disciples were all heard speaking in other languages (Acts 2).

This manifestation of tongues is not the same thing as praying in an unknown language. So what we have in the gift of tongues is the Spirit speaking a human language through us for others to understand and also praying in the Spirit in a language that others don't understand. Then there are also times when the Holy Spirit brings a message through tongues and an interpretation. These are different manifestations, and the Holy Spirit wants us to have them all.

The manifestation of these gifts is mentioned in 1 Corinthians 14. Paul was very clear that those who speak in tongues speak directly to God in mysteries that no one else understands (v. 2), but those who prophesy edify others (v. 3). Paul was thankful that he spoke in tongues in his prayers but also wanted to speak things that were understood by others in the church (vv. 18–19). Sometimes our tongues are for our own edification, and sometimes they are for the edification of others. Sometimes they are in a heavenly language that no human understands, sometimes they are a message with an interpretation, and sometimes they are an earthly language for others to hear. So the Spirit wants to build us up, and He also wants to build others up. There is value in each manifestation of the gift.

I need as much edifying as I can get, so I pray in tongues as often as I can. The Holy Spirit wants to give us the encouragement, affirmation, and strength we need, and in measures that are greater than our words can handle. As we're praying in tongues, He downloads these things into our spirit, builds us up, and accomplishes more in our lives than we can see.

How to Receive the Baptism of the Spirit

There's a wonderful verse in Jude, a very short book with only one chapter. Verses 20 and 21 say, "But you, beloved, build yourselves up in your most holy faith. Pray in the Holy Spirit. Keep yourselves in the love of God while you are waiting for the mercy of our Lord Jesus Christ, which leads to eternal life." That encourages me to pray in the Spirit, but it also tells me there is something we need to do to remain in Him. We need to deliberately lean back into Him to keep ourselves in the love of God. If you don't know how to do that, talk to Him about it.

If you've never been baptized in the Spirit or don't know how to receive the gift of speaking in tongues, just ask. Everyone who believes has been born of the Spirit (John 7:38–39), but Scripture also points to being filled with power both as a separate event (Acts 1:4, 8; 4:31; 19:2, 6) and an ongoing process (Acts 13:52; Eph. 5:18). Jesus was talking about the Holy Spirit when He told His followers to ask and receive:

> Ask, and it will be given to you; seek, and you will find; knock, and it will be opened to you. For everyone who asks receives, and he who seeks finds, and to him who knocks it will be opened. If a son asks for bread from any of you who is a father, will you give him a stone? Or if he asks for a fish, will you give him a serpent instead of a fish? Or if he asks for an egg, will you offer him a scorpion? If you then, being evil, know how to give good gifts to your children, how much more will your heavenly Father give the Holy Spirit to those who ask Him?
> —LUKE 11:9–13

If you're just waiting for this gift to come to you one day, you might be waiting a long time. In the kingdom things come by asking in faith and receiving. The Spirit is waiting for you to ask Him to baptize you. There's no need to worry that you might get some other spirit. The Father gives good gifts; He won't give you something dangerous when you have asked Him for something good. If you come asking the Father to baptize you with the Spirit, He will do it. And you have to take it by faith. Just as you receive salvation by faith, you can receive the baptism of the Holy Spirit by faith. You can open your mouth and speak with new tongues.

We see evidence of this over and over again in Scripture. People were baptized in the Holy Spirit and spoke with other tongues. The gift of speaking in a prayer language to God is for all who will receive it. God definitely wants to give that to you. It's how the Spirit intercedes through you and for you.

Ask for that. "Whatever things you ask when you pray, believe that you will receive them, and you will have them" (Mark 11:24). Don't ask and then strain for it: "Please, please, please. I'm trying, Lord, but I don't feel anything." Ask believing you have received it already, knowing it's the will of God for you. "Daddy, I would like the baptism of the Holy Spirit. I would like to speak with new tongues." Take it by faith, and begin to speak. At first your strange words may sound like you're making them up. You might wonder if it's the Holy Spirit or just your own attempts. But if you've asked for something good and are believing in faith you received it, just keep speaking. After a few minutes you will likely feel the Holy Spirit empowering your words from within your belly. That's what happened in Acts again and again. It's part of the normal Christian life.

The Purpose of Praying in the Spirit

Paul wrote that those who pray in an unknown tongue edify themselves (1 Cor. 14:4). We need all the building up we can get. If we don't know how to pray in the Spirit, we have to look to other people to build us up. Other believers can be encouraging and affirming, but people should not be our only source of affirmation. It is not a weakness to need encouragement; the Holy Spirit wants to be the One who meets that need in our hearts. He may use other people, but He also wants to encourage and strengthen us directly. Whenever we're weary physically, emotionally, or any other way, He is there to build us up. So when you pray in an unknown tongue, it's actually the Holy Spirit praying through you and for you. He is setting things up for your good.

The Holy Spirit wants to speak kind words to us. "Heaviness in the heart of man makes it droop, but a good word makes it glad" (Prov. 12:25). The Holy Spirit tells us not to be anxious about anything, but with prayer and supplication to make our requests known to God (Phil. 4:6). He wants to guide our hearts with peace. When I used to ask the Holy Spirit to speak to me, I would expect Him to tell me what was wrong with me. Then He would often surprise me with kind words. Yes, He will point out things that need correcting sometimes, but He does not spend all His time on correction. He loves to lavish love on His people. Ephesians 3:16–19 says we need supernatural strength to be able to receive all the love He wants to give. Don't be surprised if you come to the Holy Spirit in a time of weakness, feeling hypocritical, and all you hear from Him is, "There you are! I'm so happy to see you!" You may not feel as if you deserve it, but that isn't the point. He knows you don't deserve it; that's what mercy and forgiveness are all about.

If you've done something wrong, and you know it, church is exactly the right place to be. Confess your sin, and then open your mouth, begin to pray in unknown tongues, and let the Holy Spirit build you up and encourage you. He will blow away all the condemnation and keep your gaze fixed on the Him, who can help you.

There is a war going on, and the Holy Spirit can see the terrain better than you can. He knows strategies, where the enemy is positioned, and what he will attempt next. As you begin to pray in the Spirit, He swats away the weapons raised against you. If you find yourself in a non-praying mood, get up and open your mouth anyway. Pray in faith no matter what you're feeling. Begin by speaking in tongues and attaching faith to them. Some people babble away in tongues without any faith, but everything in the kingdom comes by faith. It isn't a matter of saying all the right words and praying the right prayers; the point is to engage your mind in faith while praying in the Spirit. As you do, the Holy Spirit is dealing with things you can't even see.

When I was younger, I would read the scripture about the Holy Spirit making intercession for us with groanings that cannot be uttered and be worried that prayer in the Spirit was not tongues at all, only groans. But this is just another aspect of praying in the Spirit. Just as we read about unknown tongues and about known tongues that are supernaturally given to the speaker or translated for the hearer, we also read about the Holy Spirit's groanings. You will experience this sometimes as you're praying for people or a specific situation. You won't necessarily know what the groans mean, but they come out of the depths of your spirit. When you experience them in prayer, know that the Holy Spirit feels deep and compassionate about the situation and is communing with the Father for His will to be done in the situation or the life of the person for whom you're praying.

Romans 8:27 says, "He who searches the hearts knows what the mind of the Spirit is, because He intercedes for the saints according to the will of God." The Father knows perfectly what is on the heart of the Spirit because they are One. There is no barrier to the Holy Spirit's prayer. So when you are praying in the Spirit, engaging in faith and allowing groanings to come up, perfect intercession is happening. The will of God is being accomplished. It's a very exciting moment.

We Are All Intercessors

I believe the body of Christ has too often relegated groaning prayers to something a few strange intercessors do. The church has not always understood that everyone who has the Holy Spirit is anointed and qualified to come into agreement with God and make intercession. Scripture says that both the Holy Spirit and Jesus are interceding for us (Rom. 8:26, 34). If Jesus is living in you—if "it is no longer [you] who live, but Christ who lives in [you]—you are by nature an intercessor (Gal. 2:20). Your identity is in

Him, and He is seated in heavenly places at the right hand of the Father interceding for all the saints. "As He is, so are we in this world" (1 John 4:17). All of us are intercessors.

The Spirit of God wants to help us make a shift in our thinking. There has been too much segregation in the body. We have different gifts, but we've also become too specialized, assuming some things are for a select group of people. He wants to birth the greatest move of God the world has ever seen, and He is calling forth an intercessor's heart in each of us to dream His dreams and agree with His groanings and unknown tongues. The Holy Spirit will do what He longs to do through the prayers of His people.

As a young woman, I dreaded the thought of being an intercessor. I went to a church where women weren't allowed to preach or lead, but they could go to prayer meetings. In fact, that's pretty much all women did. But God began teaching me about intercession, and it was different from what I assumed it would be. The beautiful ladies in the prayer group had some wonderful encounters with God.

I still didn't want to identify solely with intercessors. It didn't seem very exciting to be relegated to this while others did miracles and won souls. But Jesus is our great intercessor. We have to realize intercession isn't a separate ministry but something we are all called to. Some people may have a specific calling to intercede, and they can have extremely powerful ministries. They often manifest the fruit of the Spirit in remarkable ways and see people healed and mountains moved even though you never see them publicly. But the Holy Spirit began to do a work in my heart and showed me that unless I was willing to lay my life down in intercession, I wasn't qualified for anything else in the kingdom. Without love we have nothing, and the heart of an intercessor is moved by love. There's no public glory in that ministry. Love is its only motivation. I really believe the body of Christ needs to wake up and share that burden.

You have probably sensed the Holy Spirit's promptings to intercede many times, though you may not have recognized it; sometimes people interpret them as random thoughts. But I've found that when I turn those sudden promptings into prayer, God uses them to intervene and accomplish His purposes. I often find out afterward why I was prompted to pray, and you will learn the results too when you answer the prompt to intercede. If you ask Him, He will show you visions not only of what to pray for but also of what He did through it. God's eyes roam to and fro throughout the world looking for those whose hearts are completely His (2 Chron. 16:9), and sometimes His search is for someone to pray for a specific situation. If we leave that only to people designated as intercessors, the will of God will not be fully accomplished. Intercession is for everyone.

Our lives are not about our own promotion; they are about His. We have to begin to recognize that our lives are to serve Him and come into agreement with the Holy Spirit. We are part of a global team called the body of Christ, and our mission is to see God's kingdom come on earth as it is in heaven. That won't happen through the prayers of a few, but it will if we all partner with the Holy Spirit to intercede for it.

Sometimes the Holy Spirit wants to birth things in you

through intercession. Once I was sobbing as I was praying before a meeting, just interceding. I call this liquid prayers (Lam. 2:19). That night was one of the biggest moves of God I had ever seen up to that time. People flooded the altar in repentance. A young man came up to testify in front of two thousand people that he had stuttered all his life and couldn't possibly speak in front of a crowd, and he spoke perfectly. Deaf ears opened. Many were weeping at the way God's miracle-working power had healed them and taken away their pain.

Those kinds of prayers don't happen all the time, and they are certainly not something we should try to muster up. But sometimes tears flow as you're moving with the Spirit. As we give ourselves to Him in intercession and lean on His strength, He moves through us with His emotions and desires.

Romans 8:28 is one of the best-known verses in the Bible, and it was written in this context of prayer. "We know that all things work together for good to those who love God, to those who are called according to His purpose." I've discovered something glorious that happens when we pray in the Spirit in faith. It's only when I have been very deliberate to exercise the gift of tongues that I've seen advancement happen in my life. Sometimes I've been complacent and prayed only a little, but in this recent season I've been encouraged to pray regularly and intensely in the Spirit. I find that I can't afford to pray less than half an hour a day in the Spirit because I need so much help, and I want to see the kingdom established in the earth. A lot of people have time to read the newspaper or watch TV for half an hour but not to come into agreement with God in groanings too deep for words. I'm the other way around, and I hope you are too. I have to ask Him to use my mouth to pray what's on His heart. He uses our intercession to work all things together for good.

Intercession not only advances His kingdom, but it also draws you closer to the Holy Spirit. Partnering with the Holy Spirit increases your intimacy with Him. Tom and I have been married for twenty-five years, and I talk to him a lot about all the different things I need. He is constantly helping me, and he's very patient when he does it. But if our relationship consisted of nothing but my telling him what I need, it would be a pretty shallow relationship. That's how it is with God too. He wants to take your relationship with Him to a much deeper level. He delights in meeting your needs, and He loves taking all your anxieties on Himself and encouraging you. But you need more than that, and He wants more. He wants you to hear what is on His heart. Praying in the Spirit opens your heart to what He wants to share with you.

When I pray in tongues with my mind engaged and have covered all of my requests, I try to go on a little longer. That's when I suddenly find myself getting fresh initiatives about what to do. This creativity directly correlates with the amount of time I spend praying in the Spirit. The Holy Spirit begins releasing the Father's plans to me. So instead of being anxious and wondering what I'm going to do in a certain situation, I give Him my anxious thoughts and pray in the Spirit, and new ideas come up—not just answers to my problems but also fresh insights about things to accomplish. He fills my heart with joy about what He is going to do.

The Holy Spirit Prays Through You for You

The Spirit prays for you. God wants to lift you above all the confusion, anxiety, and worries and remove what wants to steal your peace. Suddenly you can see what you're called to, and you can see His plans for the earth. You get His ideas and are led to agree with and declare them. You will be burdened with all the "shoulds" and feel the weight of them, but if you allow the Spirit to pray through you and deal with everything you can't see, you will be strengthened and encouraged. Your heart was not made to carry stress and burdens; it was made for righteousness, peace, and joy. Your ability to release burdens is directly related to how much time you pray. Instead of being weighed down, you will rise up, sing, and rejoice.

The Holy Spirit wants you to recognize that whatever you are walking through, He is not discouraged. He is excited for you because it will work out for your good. He is praying to the Father about the divine recompense that you'll receive as you turn your anxieties and pain over to Him. As I pray in tongues, I imagine the Holy Spirit saying, "Oppression, leave her alone! Confusion, go! I banish you. Let her see the truth of the situation and know the hope of her calling. Katherine, be free to dream the dreams of God." I picture Him making declarations over my family, my circumstances, and my city. I know that the powerful King is working through me and for me, and as you pray in the Spirit, He will do that for you too.

You may pray for your own agenda, but when praying in tongues the Holy Spirit will pray what He wants. You can trust that His prayers are the will of the Father. If you're caught in deception or have a distorted view, He will pray what is needed and eventually bring you into the light.

Some people think others' prayers are their only hope. We need to pray for one another, and intercessors who support a ministry and its leaders in prayer do an important work. However, if you neglect prayer, expecting others to carry the load, you're apathetic. And if you neglect prayer because you think they are not effective, you need to start exercising faith in the Holy Spirit. Intercession is a privilege we get to enjoy, and just thinking about it encourages me to open my mouth and pray in tongues so the Holy Spirit can be praying *for* me and *through* me.

Intercession is necessary. We have a part to play in seeing God's will done. The Holy Spirit says, "Get up. Give Me your anxious thoughts, and stand up as a mighty warrior. You are more than a conqueror. Use the weapons of your warfare. Pray in the Spirit. Make declarations. Ask, and you will receive." God rarely accomplishes anything in this world unilaterally, apart from His people. He often initiates prophecies and prayers, but He puts them in the hands of human beings to declare and pray before He intervenes. Humanity looks at God and says, "Why don't You do something?" God looks at His people and says, "Why don't *you* do something?" Intercede. Open your mouth, and let the Lord put His words into it.

You have a choice. God has put life and death before you and is saying, "Choose life." You have to do that on a daily basis. It's not a one-time decision; even after being made into a new creation, you have a free will and exercise it daily. You can choose life by humbly recognizing that you don't have everything it takes to get through life on your own. You are joined with God and called to partner with the Holy Spirit. Without Him you can do nothing, but you can do all things through Christ (Phil. 4:13). Open your mouth, and let the Holy Spirit pray through you. He wants to intercede through you and give you breakthrough as you come into agreement with Him. He gave us the keys of the kingdom and the signature of His name for that reason. It's a divine invitation, and the Lord wants to respond to it because we are about to enter into something glorious.

Chapter 11

THE SPIRIT OF LOVE

A COUPLE CAME UP to me after a service and told me their younger daughter had given her heart to Christ that morning. That was wonderful news, and I rejoiced with them. But the main reason they had come up to speak to me was to tell me the story of their other daughter, who had given birth three years earlier to a premature baby. The baby had complications, and the situation didn't look good. In her distress this couple's daughter had been praying, "God, if you're real, give me a sign." She and her husband met some people from our church in an elevator who reached out to them with the love of Christ. They felt led to pray for them and the child and to bless them with some money, saying, "Your baby is going to be fine." The baby was healed, and three years later the child is in perfect health and doing well. The parents had come to tell me their entire family had been changed.

I enjoy hearing those kinds of stories because they are demonstrations of God's love to people who are desperate for real love. We hear stories of our church members prophesying in coffee shops and going to hospitals to pray for healing, and the miracles that come out of those efforts are amazing. It's so beautiful to see the love of God being poured out as the church becomes outward focused. Revival is not church-centric. It is not about improving church life. It is going out and bringing in the harvest, taking the glory everywhere in fellowship with the Holy Spirit, delivering the message with demonstrations of the Holy Spirit's power, and letting what is being poured out on us be poured out on others outside the church. In fact, sharing what God is doing is what continues to spark revival. The Holy Spirit has already begun pouring Himself out in revival, but He is preparing us for even more. He is fine-tuning us to get us ready.

That is why I've been encouraging people to read the Word of God, to pray the apostolic prayers, and to feast on His Word. It has the power to change us. The Word of God is like a holy chiropractor that adjusts us to be in perfect alignment. My desire is to see people who love the Word not with knowledge that puffs up but with humility that says, "This is food for my soul."

Humility is a key for revealing God's heart to the world, and everything we do must come from a place of love. When it comes to manifesting the Holy Spirit people don't want to hear from know-it-alls who are full of themselves and thinking more about communicating their message than about the people to whom they are ministering. They want to be seen with eyes of love and respect, treated as those who are made in the image of God. It takes humility to approach people with that attitude, a humility that comes from knowing we love "because He first loved us"

(1 John 4:19). Humility is necessary to share God's love with those around you.

I have seen the power of love at work again and again. My first book, *Living in the Miraculous,* was all about the way in which God's love is demonstrated through the supernatural. I see it when the Lord gives a prophetic word to someone who has not yet been saved and speaks into that person's value and desires. I've seen it when people feel respected and open up their hearts to receive Christ. Ministering to people while having a judgmental attitude that says they have something wrong with them and you're going to fix it turns them away. You'll reap what you sow; that judgment will come back to you in the measure you used. The people you minister to will react defensively, closing their hearts to the love of God. But if you approach people with humility, seeing them from God's perspective, they open up and receive what He has for them. Ministry can be powerful, but love is what matters. Without love we are nothing. Love will never fail.

As a mother I take it personally when someone does something for my children to help or encourage them. It means so much to me, and I receive the gesture of love as though it were shown to me directly. If they have blessed my children, they have blessed me. I believe the Father too takes it personally when we reach out in the power of His Spirit, especially to those who don't yet know Jesus and need to experience God's love in order to become reconciled to Him. Every time you care about someone else more than your own comfort, it warms His heart. Jesus said, "As you have done it for one of the least of these brothers of Mine, you have done it for Me" (Matt. 25:40). The Holy Spirit loves to minister through us with genuine love to those who need His touch.

A Revival of Love

The Holy Spirit partners with those whose gaze is fixed on Him in truth and love. One of the passages I've feasted on recently is from 1 Peter:

> Finally, be all of one mind, be loving toward one another, be gracious, and be kind. Do not repay evil for evil, or curse for curse, but on the contrary, bless, knowing that to this you are called, so that you may receive a blessing. For "He who would love life and see good days, let him keep his tongue from evil, and his lips from speaking deceit."
>
> —1 PETER 3:8–10

What struck me in this passage is the power that is available to us through the Holy Spirit to live a life of love. You can prophesy with incredible accuracy, but if you don't have love, it's nothing (1 Cor. 13:1–2). You can manifest the miraculous power of God in all kinds of signs and wonders, but if you don't know who you are and don't display good, godly character when you move in power, you become dangerous. The Holy Spirit doesn't just want to manifest power. He wants to manifest Jesus, and Jesus is love. When Jesus is lifted up and magnified in our lives, people will be drawn to Him. We get to demonstrate to the world around us what He looks like, and by His power we manifest His love.

I love the fact that this passage from 1 Peter tells us to pay people back with a blessing rather than an insult. We have subtle ways of getting around this; I've done it myself. When someone does something mean, we want to be Christian enough not to repay it outwardly, but we inwardly put up a wall to distance ourselves. But when we start engaging with the pattern of the world and step out of love, we grieve the Holy Spirit, and He jealously yearns to help us recognize what is happening. Those subtle barbs at the people who have hurt us don't fit with who we are anymore. We are brand-new creations with the capacity to love even our enemies. In our new nature we can do good to those who are nasty to us. We get to bless people because of the revelation of God's love continually being revealed to us by the Holy Spirit.

I used to think that was so unfair. If I bless people who hurt me, how will they know to stop? If I pray for them, shouldn't I pray that God would convict them of their sin so they can see how wrong they are? My whole approach, even if it was just inside my own heart, revolved around the offense. Sure, I would pray for them—for God to bless them with conviction and repentance. But I found it really difficult to want to see them blessed because they might misinterpret the blessings that came their way as signs that God was OK with their bad behavior. But I discovered that I can trust the Holy Spirit to handle those things. He's actually on my side. Instead of praying, "Lord, bless those people who are being so nasty," I dropped the "nasty" and just prayed for God to love them, give them favor, and bless their marriages, families, and finances. I can trust

Him to give them exactly what they need at exactly the right time.

That does something powerful. It releases you. When you retaliate, no matter how subtly, you are stepping out of the Holy Spirit's ways. Every time you see the person, the pain resurfaces. But when you begin to move in the opposite spirit from what feels natural, the enemy can't drag you down. You no longer have any need to try to judge what they've done. You are free to love, forgive, and bless. God is well able to sort things out in their lives on His own.

The passage goes on to describe what it looks like to walk in the opposite spirit:

> "For the eyes of the Lord are on the righteous, and His ears are open to their prayers; but the face of the Lord is against those who do evil." Who is he who will harm you if you follow that which is good? But even if you suffer for the sake of righteousness, you are blessed. "Do not be afraid of their terror, do not be troubled." But sanctify the Lord God in your hearts. Always be ready to give an answer to every man who asks you for a reason for the hope that is in you, with gentleness and fear. Have a good conscience so that evildoers who speak evil of you and falsely accuse your good conduct in Christ may be ashamed.
> —1 Peter 3:12–16

You don't need to be worried about the consequences of walking in the spirit opposite from your natural desires. You are no longer subject to the rules of the natural world. God is with you. He will take care of you and whomever you pray for and bless. The Holy Spirit wants to remind you constantly that you are not normal anymore.

Have compassion on people who are mean to you because they don't know what they are doing. They have no idea they are messing with the apple of God's eye. You can pray as Jesus did—for God to forgive them because they know not what they do. God is going to take care of you, but they really need prayer.

This attitude frees you up to love people, which is the true heart behind revival. God's great move will be an out-pouring of love because that's who He is. God is pouring out His Spirit on all flesh and will use anyone who will yield to His leading. He's going to reveal His glory—and His heart—through those who can humble themselves in love.

The Power of Humility

As was mentioned previously, humility is necessary for sharing the life-changing love of God. Humility is walking in submission to the character of Christ. What does that look like? For starters it means coming before Him daily and saying, "Lord, today I consider myself dead to sin but alive to You. Thank You that I have been set free from me! You are my Lord. I choose to submit to You. I thank You, Holy Spirit, that I have everything pertaining to life and godliness. Teach me Your ways, and lead me in Your paths. I want to walk with You today, fully aware of the grace of the Lord Jesus, Your great love for me, and Your fellowship, Holy Spirit, that I might manifest the character of Christ."

Such selfless thinking is the opposite of what our world considers to be culturally acceptable. In Australia we love the song "What About Me" by Garry Frost and Frances Swan. It moans about how unfair life is and asks the question, "It's fine for everyone else, but what about me?" It may be a catchy song, but it doesn't represent kingdom culture. It represents the opposite of Christlikeness. The moment we say, "What about me?," we step outside of grace and into our own ways. His way is to say, "I'm going to care more for other people." If you humbly follow the Holy Spirit's leading into a life of respecting and honoring others above yourself, you'll be blessed. When we choose to consider ourselves dead and see things from a kingdom perspective, all these things get added without our having to strive for them. When you "seek first the kingdom of God and His righteousness," all these things will be added to you, and the question "What about me?" becomes irrelevant (Matt. 6:33).

We saw in 1 Peter 3:9 that we are not to repay evil for evil but rather pay people back with a blessing. That's what God did for us, and it's what He calls us to do for others. This is challenging because it isn't a natural human response. The flesh wants to respond in pride, which is the opposite of humility.

I'm diligent in sowing pain in faith. If something bad happens that causes me pain, shame, or disgrace, I know God will give me double recompense if I believe Him for it. Isaiah 61:7 says, "Instead of your shame you shall have double honor, and instead of humiliation they shall rejoice over their portion. Therefore, in their land they shall possess a double portion; everlasting joy shall be theirs." Zechariah 9:12 promises the same thing: "Return to your stronghold, prisoners who now have hope. Today I declare that I will return to you a double portion." Some people think, "That's great for innocent victims, but I'm the one who caused my pain and shame. I deserve it." But these words were originally given to people who had been disciplined for their own sins and mistakes. Even so, God still promised to doubly restore their blessing.

The Holy Spirit wants to help us live as the redeemed by reminding us of the truth so we will respond in hope, faith, and humility rather than reverting back to old patterns. Whatever pain or shame you've experienced, regardless of whose fault it is, you can take it to God in faith and say, "Thank You, Father. This is divine currency that I can exchange. I give You this pain and thank You for the exchange rate of heaven—double recompense. I give up any need to retaliate, and instead I sow it and thank You for the double honor!" I've seen Him answer this prayer again and again. It takes away any need I feel to defend myself. I don't need to pray that they would be "blessed with conviction." God has promised to bless me, and that's all I need to know.

God is trustworthy. He knows how to work everything out in just the right way. My job when interacting with other people is to forsake pride and embrace humility—to love, forgive, bless, and trust Him to work all things together for the good of those who love Him and are called according to His purpose (Rom. 8:28). I can release everything to Him because He is faithful and true. The Holy Spirit works things out gloriously.

Our ways of dealing with people can seem perfectly

reasonable to us. It may seem right to me to treat people differently when they wrong me. But Proverbs 14:12 tells us, "There is a way that seems right to a man, but its end is the way of death." The Holy Spirit's way is radical forgiveness, and it is so much better. I'm not saying you should never have a heart-to-heart conversation with someone to resolve a conflict. That's biblical and right, but the motivation must not be to cause pain in return. The Holy Spirit wants to help us first to forgive and place our trust in God. Then, if necessary, the Holy Spirit can help us have a discussion without any agenda other than to love that person well. In humility and by the power of the Holy Spirit we can leave the rest to God. We can then turn our attention to the Holy Spirit and fix our focus on something pure, lovely, noble, praiseworthy, or of good report.

I believe that this kind of humility is a prerequisite for having the power of God be made known through us. If God gave us the impressive gifts without humility, there would be a lot of dangerous people out there misrepresenting Him—people who are constantly trying to get their own needs met and who use gifts for their own selfish purposes rather than out of love. Power and love flow together, and it's impossible to have real love without humility. It's an integral part of what God is doing in us to prepare us for increasing revival.

I was desperate for God when I was a teenager. I would go down to the altar crying out for God to humble me. I was afraid of being proud because I knew pride comes before a fall, and I wanted to avoid that. A wise counselor told me, "You probably shouldn't pray that, honey. Maybe pray for a humble attitude instead." So I prayed for a humble attitude because I knew God wants us to walk in humility. The reality is that you can't make yourself humble, but you can receive the humility of Christ. You can ask God to teach you how to walk it out and show you what it looks like. Humility isn't thinking poorly of yourself; that's insecurity. I have heard it said that true humility is not thinking less of yourself; it is thinking of yourself less.[1] We will walk in true humility when we embrace the nature of Christ in us. The result will be a true compassion and respect for others that will cause you to overflow with love that is put into action. When you know you don't have anything to prove because you are dead and Christ now lives in you, you will naturally walk in humility.

When Tom and I were courting, I was fiddling around on the piano on his twenty-first birthday. Tom's father came downstairs and complimented me on my playing. I didn't know how to handle a compliment, so I said something like, "Oh, I'm really terrible; I don't play very well." Downplaying a compliment can be done out of insecurity or be a way to fish for more compliments. I should have thanked him for his kindness because that's really what it was. I've since learned that compliments are not necessarily even about you. They mean someone has made an effort to encourage you. A humble response is not to deny that gift or to say, "Yes, I really am good." Humility values that person's generous spirit and accepts his or her encouragement. A simple thank-you is a humble response.

When some people receive a compliment, they say, "It's not me; it's God." Bill Johnson says whenever someone says that to him, he tells them, "It wasn't *that* good."[2] Corrie ten Boom said that when people gave her compliments, she would accept them. Afterward she would go home, gather up all the compliments in her head, bring them before the Lord like a beautiful bunch of roses, and offer them up to Him.[3] I think that's beautiful. For me, as God has been enlarging my influence, I have been really challenged on this point. Giving God all the honor and glory needs to be more than a theology we know about; it must become our daily practice. I need to do what Corrie ten Boom did. Pride is subtle and can easily creep in. If we make a daily practice of consciously giving God all the glory for every good thing He gives us, we can keep our hearts clear. Regularly recognizing His majesty and goodness helps us remember that it is all about Him, and focusing on the person who is complimenting you rather than on your own insecurities expresses humility in love.

A Life of Influence

The Spirit is calling you to a life of influence, but you can have real influence only with the humility of love. You cannot help people when you are trying to fix them because if you're trying to fix them, you've already judged that they need your fixing. The Holy Spirit's desire is to touch people so they will experience life, healing, and love. He does the fixing because He is the only One who really knows what needs to be fixed. Your job is to remove any walls that might inhibit His life, healing, and love from flowing through you. The Holy Spirit wants to help us walk in the reality of what love looks like so we can drop all our walls, move in the opposite spirit of the world's ways, demonstrate love through our daily lives, and allow people to see God through us.

The writer of Hebrews wanted his readers to be careful because there was a real risk they might fall into a trap. "Pursue peace with all men, and the holiness without which no one will see the Lord, watching diligently so that no one falls short of the grace of God, lest any root of bitterness spring up to cause trouble, and many become defiled by it" (Heb. 12:14–15). It was important for them to do everything possible to live at peace with one another and pursue holiness, which is not a list of legalistic rules but actually the character of God Himself. God gives us grace to manifest His character. Paul said to pursue peace as much as it depends on you (Rom. 12:18)—meaning it may not always depend on you. You won't be able to win everyone over. But set your heart on forgiving and releasing everyone, knowing that the love of the Holy Spirit brings down walls and conquers hard hearts.

The Holy Spirit wants your world to be thoroughly peaceful, inside and out, in your own heart and mind and in your relationships. He wants you to have supernatural peace. He wants people to be able to encounter the Prince of Peace when they meet you.

Do people encounter the peace of Jesus when they meet you? Do they encounter His love? His joy? If not the Holy Spirit wants to change that. The Holy Spirit wants you to manifest Him every day in your world. Not only is this possible; it's your divine inheritance. But it requires being submitted to the Holy Spirit and letting the Word instruct you daily. It's quite exciting to wake up in the morning and feast on the Word to see what you look like. If you aren't manifesting the things Jesus did—healing and delivering in a completely loving, peaceful, forgiving way—it doesn't mean you're a bad Christian. It means you've forgotten what you look like. Choose to say yes to what Scripture says about you. Thank the Holy Spirit for showing you and walking with you to help you live it out. Set your mind on Him, and walk in His life and peace. Turn away from the patterns of the world and "be transformed by the renewing of your mind" (Rom. 12:2). Let the Holy Spirit empower you to be a manifestation of the life, healing, and love of Jesus.

The Simplicity of a Child

The Lord is looking for people who will walk in genuine, childlike humility:

> At that time the disciples came to Jesus, saying, "Who is the greatest in the kingdom of heaven?" Jesus called a little child to Him and set him in their midst, and said, "Truly I say to you, unless you are converted and become like little children, you will not enter the kingdom of heaven. Therefore whoever humbles himself like this little child is greatest in the kingdom of heaven."
> —Matthew 18:1–4

Little children just believe. If a trusted person tells them something new, they just believe what they are told. True, childlike humility involves trusting God's Word above our own understanding. If you want to walk in miracles, know that God is looking for people who will walk in that simplicity of spirit—who can embrace what He says with childlike faith. That kind of faith refuses to be convinced about anything other than His truth. Those who humble themselves like little children say, "Lord, You are God, and You will do it." They don't balk when He says to go heal the sick and tell people the kingdom of God has come upon them. They don't try to adjust things according to their intellectual experience. They set their faces like flint on who He is and what He has said. They are able to then share the love of God with others because they simply believe it, receive it, and share it with others.

I've seen a lot of people who once hungered for the miraculous and then started to go cold on it. Sometimes they have even seen people healed but have later experienced disappointment, wondering why healing doesn't happen all the time. They back off on their pursuit of the miraculous in order to avoid disappointment. I believe if you humble yourself as a child and continue to pursue God, that's when you begin to see the kingdom of God manifested. A skeptical mind changes its understanding of scripture in order to fit life's experiences. A childlike mind focuses on getting life experiences to line up with the truth of Scripture made known to them by the Holy Spirit. Only people who choose to live this way get to enjoy the fullness of what God wants to do through them: demonstrating His love to the world.

Jesus is "the way, the truth, and the life" (John 14:6). He is the rock. Some of us learned that as far back as Sunday school, and in the simplicity of our faith we accepted it. We saw in Scripture that everyone who came to Him for healing was healed. For everyone who had a problem, He manifested Himself as the answer. Not one time did He leave someone hanging or tell someone it was better to remain sick. Similar to little children, we can choose to believe His uncompromising goodness. Disappointments may creep in and cause many people to modify their thinking, but childlike faith insists what He said is true. The Holy Spirit wants to help you live in this childlike faith. I want to build my faith, my doctrine, and my life on Jesus just as He showed Himself to be, and I must have the Holy Spirit's help to do that. I don't ever want my teaching to prepare people for disappointment. There's no logic in that. I want to build confidence in who Jesus is as revealed to me through His Word and His Spirit, and trust that He will do what He said He would do.

I believe there is hope—and His name is Jesus. Without Him we have nothing. The moment we start to compromise on who Jesus is and forget that He is the same yesterday, today, and forever, we're on unstable ground (Heb. 13:8). Jesus is the rock (1 Cor. 10:4), and the Holy Spirit is with us to help us continually see who Jesus is. The winds and floods may come, but houses built on the rock stand firm. We have to make a choice of whether to build on the rock or on sand. (See Matthew 7:24–27.) If we entertain thoughts that maybe He isn't as good as He said or that He doesn't heal as He did in Scripture, we are building on sand. That's very unstable ground. Instead if we submit to the Holy Spirit's help and in humility say, "Lord, I believe," and then follow through with our thinking, we will see the manifestation of Jesus the miracle worker in us and through us. When we submit to Him, He is able to demonstrate the love of God through us.

The Holy Spirit wants to help you take captive any thoughts that try to exalt themselves against the knowledge of Christ. That doesn't mean only thoughts that are obviously evil. It means any thought that does not line up with who Jesus is. When you receive a bad diagnosis, for example, all the thoughts about what could happen or how badly it could go are exalting themselves against Jesus, your healer. They have to be cast down and replaced with truth. The Holy Spirit will help you if you ask Him. All the questions about what's going to happen, when, where, how, and why are not valid questions. The only real issue is *who*? Jesus delights to manifest Himself to you through the Holy Spirit as the One who works miracles, as the God of breakthrough. That's the kind of thought that belongs in your mind.

The Holy Spirit wants to take up full residence in your brain—your thoughts, your will, your emotions. He wants them all. You have a choice every moment of every day. Are you going to realize He is wiser than you and submit to Him just like a child? Or are you going to choose your own way? One way leads to life and peace; the other to confusion, heaviness, and even death. Choose life!

Our Dance With the Lord

I see a wonderful illustration of this submission in my marriage. Call me a traditionalist if you will, but I still believe in wives submitting to their husbands. I also believe in husbands loving their wives and laying down their lives for them, just as Christ loves the church and sacrificed Himself for us. There's a beauty in this design that, when it works the way it should, actually serves my best interests. I believe Tom has been given an anointing to protect me, and if he tells me not to travel somewhere, I need to be able to accept that God is either speaking through him or will speak to him to change his mind. Most of the time when this happened, I've found out later that there was a good reason. On the rare occasion when I've felt that God wanted me to do something and Tom didn't, I've prayed about it, and the Lord has changed one of our minds.

Tom still has to tell me sometimes to stop getting emotionally drawn into the dramas in which people want to involve me. I can offer advice and prayer and help, but then I must deliberately embrace righteousness, peace, and joy, realigning my inner world by faith with that of the kingdom of heaven. He knows me well enough to know I will be affected and lose sleep if I allow myself to be drawn into the drama. He is looking out for my welfare. I think that's a beautiful picture of what the Holy Spirit does for us. We go to do something, and He says, "No, that will not be good for you." He has our best interests in mind. When we're struggling with our thoughts, we need to be able to say, "OK, You're Lord. I'm going to humble myself and acknowledge that Your ways are better. You instruct me only in ways that bring me life because You are for me, and You are always good." We need to declare what we know to be true: that we will see His goodness in the land of the living, that our hope in Him will not disappoint, that when we walk in submission to Him as Lord of our thoughts, He gives us peace (Ps. 27:13; Rom. 5:5).

When you trust the leading of the Holy Spirit in your everyday life, life with Him becomes a beautiful dance. When a bride and groom dance, the groom leads—otherwise they would step on each other's toes—but everyone marvels at the beauty of them moving as one. When we dance with the Holy Spirit by following His lead in our everyday lives, we become so well tuned to His movements that following Him becomes natural, and we move as one. We can feel Him. In Him we live and move and have our being.

There is no formula for walking in miracles. The Holy Spirit is not formulaic with us. He is love; He is relational. He wants us to draw close to Him in fellowship and intimacy, and He wants that experience of love to spill over into our relationship with other people and our ministry to them. So the way He has arranged it is for us to lean on the Holy Spirit and get our direction from Him moment by moment. We need divine eye salve to be able to see in the Spirit and live from a revelation of who He is. When we gaze at Him, surrendered in advance to whatever He tells us, we can expect Him to show us opportunities to touch lives and heal them. The question is not whether He wants to heal; it's whether we are sensitive enough to His Holy Spirit's leading, leaning on His strength, and walking in His love.

In my ministry in churches I would sometimes prophesy to everyone and be there until after midnight. That's what

I thought people were supposed to do when they ministered. As I began to grow in the things of the Spirit, God started moving in amazing, glorious miracles. I would go back to a church where I had ministered before, and all they wanted was a prophetic word. They had heard me prophesy before, so a prophetic word is what they expected. Instead of assuming I knew what the Holy Spirit wanted to do, I learned to say, "Holy Spirit, what do You want to do here?," and I've seen much greater results.

If we walk in humility, we will become more effective. We will spend less time doing things that seem good to us and instead will focus on what the Holy Spirit wants to do. If we allow the Holy Spirit to work deep humility and peace into our character, we will be positioned for the glorious ways He wants to move through us in the days to come. His love will flow freely to us and through us. We will not have to wonder what revival looks like because we will be living in its fullness.

Chapter 12

YOUR CLOSEST FRIEND

I WAS DRIVING TO church by myself recently and thinking about the Holy Spirit. I love being around people, but I also really enjoy the moments I get to be in the car alone. I am able to have some time alone with God, and I'll take as much of that as I can get. So as I was driving, I told the Holy Spirit how much I enjoy His companionship. I desperately want and appreciate the companionship of the Holy Spirit and need time alone with Him.

We've talked a lot about who the Holy Spirit is and how He helps us. He is there for us in times of need, and He empowers us to love others and bear fruit for His kingdom. But the Holy Spirit wants to be more than our crisis manager and our productivity manager. He wants relationship. People used to say of Kathryn Kuhlman that the Holy Spirit was her best friend.[1] I remember hearing that and thinking, "Oh, I want that!" And I do. I love that the Holy Spirit is there when we cry out for help, but the relationship is created to be so much more than that. There's another level at which He comforts and encourages as a companion; that's the best part of our relationship with

Him. If we aren't cultivating that, we're missing out on the best gift He has given us: Himself.

"A man who has friends must show himself friendly" (Prov. 18:24). When people say they don't have any friends, I encourage them to come to a meeting, eat with people, talk with them, and invite them over. Be friendly, and you'll have friends. The next line in that verse takes it deeper: "…and there is a friend who sticks closer than a brother." I love my natural family and my church family. I appreciate my friendships and have a deep sense of loyalty to my friends. However, there is no human being on this planet who completely understands me. The Holy Spirit never misunderstands us. He's the Spirit of God Himself in the perfect fellowship of the Trinity. He knows and sees every part of you. And He gets it.

In your friendship with the Holy Spirit you never need to try to justify or defend yourself. You don't have to worry that He will think badly of you. He sees you as the apple of His eye. He looks at you in light of the blood of Jesus and smiles. He says, "Angels, have a look! Aren't they beautiful? They are looking at Me!" He absolutely delights in your company.

A Perfect Hand to Hold

Many years ago Tom had an operation. It wasn't a serious operation, but I was very nervous. As I drove home after dropping him off, I said out loud, "Oh, Holy Spirit, I just want to hold Your hand!" One of my love languages is physical touch, and I felt such a need for the comfort of the Holy Spirit. When I went back to the hospital, I sat in the waiting room until he came out of surgery. I opened up one of the magazines, which I don't normally do because they can be so full of rubbish, and I saw in this one a little article written by a Catholic priest. He told the story of a little child in a big crowd who suddenly reached up to hold his father's hand. He used that as an analogy of those moments when you're feeling insecure and want to hold the hand of God. I took that as a gift from God that day. "Lord, I just said in the car that I wanted to hold Your hand, and here You are saying You want to hold my hand too!" I told Him. That was years ago, but as I was thinking about His companionship recently, I heard Him say, "You know, I really enjoy holding your hand." It melted my heart.

You might think, "That's all very sentimental, but is it true?" Yes, it's all through Scripture. Paul prayed that we would know the love of God, the grace of our Lord Jesus Christ, and the fellowship of the Holy Spirit. He prayed that we would know the height and depth and width and breadth of God's love that surpasses understanding—and that we would be supernaturally enabled to take it all in. That's a relationship that goes way beyond, "I'm there if you need Me." It's a fellowship designed to keep you in perpetual delight, peace, righteousness, and joy. The Holy Spirit is with you all the time, and He's always on your side. Isn't that wonderful?

When I first began to understand years ago that the Holy Spirit actually enjoyed being with me and was happy to see me, everything changed. My conversations with Him used to be filled with feelings of condemnation. As I began to understand the truth of what it means to live by faith in God's forgiveness and righteousness, I was able to boldly approach the throne of grace. The Bible says, "The righteous are bold as a lion" (Prov. 28:1), but until you settle in your heart that the blood of Jesus is enough to cleanse you from all unrighteousness, you won't be able to have that boldness. You won't be able to engage in your relationship with the Holy Spirit at that level of delight and joy because you'll always be wondering if everything is OK between you.

The Holy Spirit is my best friend, and He speaks to me in all sorts of ways. If you're struggling to hear God's voice, you can open up your Bible and just start reading until you get something. The Holy Spirit will speak to you there; just keep reading. He is the Word, and He wants to speak to you. Write down what He shows you, and meditate on it for the day. Talk to someone about it. It's daily bread, but very often we just leave it out there on the ground like manna that was provided but never picked up. As we read His Word, we grow accustomed to His voice.

The Holy Spirit speaks to us not only through the Word but also in a myriad of other ways. All creation declares His glory. In the Bible it says He used a donkey to speak to a prophet one day. (See Numbers 22:21–39.) He speaks through all sorts of things to encourage us and guide us.

The Lord often speaks to me by putting random songs in my mind. One day recently an old Simon and Garfunkel song started running through my head. The lyrics were about slowing down and enjoying the day instead of rushing through it.[2] I thought, "Ahh, Lord. Are you talking to me?" A little while later I was doing something else—I hadn't stopped or slowed down yet—and the song kept coming to mind. "Oh, right, Lord. I'm listening, and I'll obey." The Holy Spirit persisted until He got my attention. He will speak to you in ways that are unique to you if you'll listen expectantly. He knows what is coming in your day, and He has encouragement for you if you take the time to tune in. He wants to help.

No Better Investment

Relationships take time. In order to develop intimate fellowship with the Holy Spirit, you have to invest quality time. It doesn't matter how much you love someone; if you don't spend quality time with him, you will not experience the richness and depth that is available. In the natural you get to know people when you eat with them. It's why Jesus was so relational, and it's also why we have Communion. Jesus had all His friends there for the Last Supper. Fellowship is powerful; people reveal personal things when you get close to them. But it can't happen if you always have an agenda and are trying to be productive. Sometimes we have a lot to discuss in staff meetings, and my heart thinks, "Can't we just stop and eat together?" I want more than getting through an agenda. I want to know what's going on in people's hearts. Just as it is in the natural with our human relationships, so it is in our fellowship with the Holy Spirit. We need to slow down and spend time with Him. As we invest in our relationship with the Holy Spirit through spending quality time together, we will experience the richness and depth of the most fulfilling relationship imaginable.

I know we live in a busy world. Work is a good thing, and we are called to be fruitful. Scripture says that. God understands the busyness of life, and He wants us to keep our hands busy. But productivity isn't the Holy Spirit's priority. Relationship is. In fact, God arranged it so our fruitfulness in the kingdom is always birthed out of relationship with the Holy Spirit. Unless we make a decision to prioritize time with Him, we will continue at a surface level and miss out on some of the treasures He desires for us to experience.

I have this principle in mind during our times of corporate worship at church. That's why I like for our worship to linger just a little longer sometimes, to look a little deeper and press in a little further. The more time we take to pursue Him, the more we receive. The more we expect to see, the more He reveals. If you think about it, worship happens when the Holy Spirit reveals Jesus and we respond. But very often we begin to engage with God and think, "That was great. Let's move on." And He's thinking, "But we've only just begun!"

One time when I was away ministering, my associate pastor led the staff meeting in my absence. The day after the meeting I called a member of our church staff and asked how it went. She was new and quite sheepishly responded, "Well, it didn't go exactly as planned. The Holy Spirit came, and we couldn't get through the agenda. But don't worry; we have arranged to meet and go through it tomorrow." I was thrilled! I said, "Oh good! That's just what we need! If our leaders are encountering God, it will impact the church!" I have learned to make time with the

Holy Spirit a priority, knowing that He calls us first to relationship and intimacy and second to the work.

The Holy Spirit knows and understands your world. I used to hear stories of great men and women of God spending eight hours a day seeking the face of God. I had three young children and knew it would be physically impossible to invest that kind of time. Frustrated, I'd think, "If they spent eight hours a day and got to do a lot of great things for God, maybe I could spend a little time and do a few of those things for Him." That was my logic. Praise God, it doesn't work that way. He tells us to believe, and we can go and do the greater things, as Jesus promised (John 14:12). Spending time with Him will make us more fruitful, but He understands our limitations. He wants our heart and our fellowship, not a time sheet.

I like sleep. I'm more effective when I have eight hours; otherwise I really struggle. I think about people who sleep three hours and then get up and pray, and that's just not me. If I slept only three hours, I would need to pray all day and stay away from people. My mind and body don't function quite right when I haven't slept well. The Holy Spirit knows this about me. He also knows how many people want to talk to me, how many e-mails and phone messages I need to answer, and how I could never stop if I just kept responding to needs and requests around me. I've learned to make a choice to say, "Lord, I need to prioritize time alone with You. I need to make sure I take time to lie down in green pastures so You can restore my soul. If I lose my fellowship with You, I've lost what I am living for. Without You I can do nothing. I want to go through life abundantly fruitful, not coasting or surviving. I'm choosing to abide in You."

A Place of Delight

If you've ever found your head full of complaints, arguments, imaginary speeches you wish you could unleash on someone, or other similar sorts of distractions, remember what Scripture tells you.

> Do not fret because of evildoers, nor be jealous of those who do injustice.
> —PSALM 37:1

> Trust in the LORD, and do good; dwell in the land, and practice faithfulness.
> —PSALM 37:3

> Whatever things are true, whatever things are honest, whatever things are just, whatever things are pure, whatever things are lovely, whatever things are of good report, if there is any virtue, and if there is any praise, think on these things.
> —PHILIPPIANS 4:8

> Set your affection on things above, not on things on earth.
> —COLOSSIANS 3:2

These are good instructions. They tell you how to live life—and how to steward your thoughts. If you want to have a happy life, the Bible tells you what to do:

Trust in the LORD with all your heart, and lean
not on your own understanding; in all your ways
acknowledge Him, and He will direct your paths.
—PROVERBS 3:5–6

Don't feed on the negative. Don't let fear get the best of
you. Don't entertain gossip. Ignore everything that is not
pure and lovely and of good report. Starve the things that
war against your soul, and feed what your spirit is longing
for—the faithfulness of God. Remind yourself constantly
of His goodness. As your friend the Holy Spirit wants to
help you do this. As you partner with Him in doing so, His
friendship becomes more evident and sweeter in your life.

I love to look through my old journals and remember
what God has done. It's like discovering something exciting
all over again. "Yes, Lord! I remember what You did there.
Thank You!" I also love to spend time with friends who
talk about the great things God has done. That helps me
feed on His faithfulness, and it sparks thanksgiving in my
heart. That's how we enter His gates—with thanksgiving
in our hearts—and we enter His courts with praise (Ps.
100:4). We have daily—even moment-by-moment—choices
about what we want to focus on, and whatever we choose
is what we allow to develop in our hearts. We draw closer
to what we gaze at. When we gaze at Him and draw close,
we value and strengthen our friendship with Him.

Psalm 37 (verse 1 quoted previously in this chapter) continues with a favorite verse of many. Verses 1–3 tell us not
to fret because of evildoers but to trust in God and feed on
His faithfulness. Then this psalm says to delight ourselves

in the Lord, and He will give us the desires of our hearts (v. 4). Isn't that kind? This is not a difficult command at all. We might expect Him to tell us to do some difficult task in order to have His favor. I'd be ready to climb a mountain or swim an ocean. But He says, "Just delight in Me." Both sides of that command are gratifying. We *do* something wonderful in order to *receive* something wonderful. He is so generous.

Some people find this command a little difficult because they don't know where to begin. What does it look like to delight in the Lord? "Delight myself in the Lord? Fabulous. Let's go.... OK, Lord, I'm delighting. I'm trying. This is what I have to do to get my desires, so I'm putting in the effort. Can I have them now?" But that isn't what this verse is saying. The Holy Spirit wants us to come into a place of rest in Him and realize that He is all our heart truly desires. Once we realize He is the delight of our souls and the joy of our salvation, those other desires fade in comparison. Everything we were worrying about and striving for becomes irrelevant. In that place of rest in His arms, without any bitter thoughts or stress and with minds fixed on Him, He can drop divine invitations into our hearts. Then we dream with the Holy Spirit, and He delights to satisfy us in that partnership.

Verse 5 says, "Commit your way to the LORD; trust also in Him, and He will bring it to pass." This is a really wonderful promise. When you read the Bible, it isn't just information. It's a personal gift, a promise, an invitation. Here the invitation is to commit to Him and trust in Him, and He brings things to pass:

> He will bring forth your righteousness as the light,
> and your judgment as the noonday. Rest in the LORD,
> and wait patiently for Him; do not fret because of
> those who prosper in their way.... Those who hope
> in the LORD will inherit the earth.
>
> —PSALM 37:6–7, 9

That word *rest* actually means "to be astonished" in Hebrew.[3] We are called to live in a place of astonishment. We come into His presence in faith, boldly believing in His goodness, that His grace has cleansed us from all unrighteousness, that we've exchanged our lives for His, that we have been given the pure and holy life of Jesus, and that we can fully engage in union with God. Our lives flow from that fellowship with the Holy Spirit, in whom "we live and move and have our being" (Acts 17:28). The Holy Spirit constantly reminds us that our Father is smiling in love, that He cares about us, and that we can simply look at Him and be astonished.

As you hold the hand of the Holy Spirit and give yourself to friendship with Him, He will continue to reveal the Father and the Son, causing your heart to be so astonished that you have to pray for more strength and wisdom to receive and understand. Only He can hold you up under the weight of glory God wants to reveal to you. We take little sips and tastes sometimes, but the Holy Spirit is inviting us into a realm of glory we have not yet experienced. We need Him to sustain us there. He wants us to walk in shining glory to reveal Himself through us to the world. To the level you behold Him—and fellowship with Him—you will also reflect Him.

My prayer is that the Holy Spirit would lead you into all truth. The truth is not information; it's a person. The Holy Spirit will lead you into a revelation of Jesus so you can know and experience the fullness of His grace, know that you are cleansed from all unrighteousness by the blood of the Lamb, and live in a place of constant fellowship with Him. This is the friendship that is available to us. I pray that you would become so sensitive to His leading that everything else becomes irrelevant. All of the promises of Scripture are available to you. You can do what you see the Father doing and say what you hear Him saying. As Jesus is, so are you in this world.

I believe the Holy Spirit wants to speak to you. He is unlikely to tell you to quit your job and withdraw into the church so you can be with Him. He wants you to recognize that He is after your whole world. He wants to take over. There is a Holy Spirit awakening in our world today; I can see Him swirling over people and awakening them to His righteousness. He's awakening hearts because He knows this is what we were born for—to live like Him. You were born to rest in God so you can delight in Him and He in you. That's why Hebrews says to strive to enter into rest (Heb. 4:11). That's a strange paradox, but it's true. The enemy works hard to steal from you the life, rest, and peace you were designed for. The enemy does not want you to lean your head against the Father and hear His voice. He is terrified of your spending time alone with God; he does not want that fellowship to develop, as it is the one thing that threatens him the most. When you enter into the rest that the Holy Spirit gives, the enemy can't touch

you. He can throw things at you—"many are the afflictions of the righteous"—but he can't touch you there (Ps
34:19). The Holy Spirit is calling you to that place of deep,
satisfying friendship.

Are you ready to give yourself completely to Him?
Imagine what God will do with people who have ceased
fretting and surrendered themselves to delight in Him,
who say, "Holy Spirit, I need to know You more. I need
deeper fellowship with You so I can handle the level of
glory You want to reveal to my heart." The more you taste,
the more you hunger. The more you hunger, the more you
are filled. And the more you are filled, the more help you
need from the Holy Spirit to strengthen you in your inner-
most being. You get greater capacity to receive, and greater
glory is revealed through you to the world around you.

GOING DEEPER

YEARS AGO WHEN I was a backup singer on a worship team, I would be concentrating so much on singing the right part that I would sometimes forget I was meant to be worshipping. It's easy for a music teacher and a perfectionist to get focused on harmonies and pitch. One day I was singing away and heard the Holy Spirit say, "Who are you singing to?"

"You, Lord," I answered. But then I realized I was singing, "I love You," with my mouth but not with my heart. I absolutely loved Him in my heart, so that wasn't the problem, but I was having a conversation with Him without being conscious of what I was saying. I made a decision at that moment never to do that again. I told the Lord I never wanted to sing another worship song without being aware of to whom I was singing, the sincerity of my words, and the reality of His presence.

I imagine what that would be like with my husband. "Um, yeah, you're awesome, Tom," as I look around and occupy myself with other things. "Really great....I appreciate you so much," while I yawn and check my e-mail.

That's a bit strange, isn't it? It doesn't demonstrate sincerity or a desire for connection. That's what happens when we think we are worshipping but don't focus on God. I think that especially happens with the Holy Spirit, who can sometimes seem like the mysterious, forgotten member of the Trinity. The Father and Son can seem easier to relate to. We have natural fathers and sons in this world, so the concepts of God the Father and God the Son make sense to us. But what about the Holy Spirit? He loves our attention too, and He very often doesn't receive it.

I don't want to grieve the Holy Spirit in any way. I know He doesn't take offense easily; that's a wonderful thing about God. "God is love," and love is not easily offended (1 John 4:8; 1 Cor. 13:5). The Holy Spirit is a friend who sticks closer than a brother. Even when I have at times drifted from truth, He remained constant and kind. He is patient and understanding. He doesn't withdraw His love. We can worship by faith, believing that as we come to worship, He is always so happy to be engaging with us. Because Jesus has made us clean and pure by His blood, we can always boldly approach the throne of grace.

I want my relationship with the Holy Spirit to be about much more than coexisting. I don't want to just mentally acknowledge His presence. I want deep, close companionship; the fullness of His power and love; His guidance and direction; His comfort and counsel; and so much more. I want to know and be deeply, passionately in love with the One who knows and is deeply, passionately in love with me. I want to do life with Him to fulfill every inch of my destiny and see His kingdom come on earth just as it is in heaven. I want to see His glory.

You wouldn't be reading this book if you didn't want these things too. This is what your heart was made for and what you've been longing for. The wonderful news is that the Holy Spirit wants to help you with everything. He wants to partner with you even more than you want to partner with Him. He wants your destiny in Him to be thoroughly, gloriously fulfilled.

Are you ready? The Holy Spirit wants to speak to your heart. He wants to encourage you, and He wants to refresh you. He wants to supernaturally expand your capacity to receive His love and demonstrate it to others. He wants you to move in His power. He wants to take you higher and higher into absolute, overwhelming joy. There is fullness of joy in His presence, and that's where you get to stand—you and Him together. A life surrendered to Him will change the world forever.

NOTES

CHAPTER 1: GOD THE FATHER, SON, AND HOLY SPIRIT

1. "Calling God 'Abba, Father,'" The High Calling, accessed December 12, 2016, https://www.theologyofwork.org/the-high -calling/daily reflection/calling-god-abba-father-1.

CHAPTER 2: THE FELLOWSHIP OF THE HOLY SPIRIT

1. Blue Letter Bible, s.v. "*pneuma*," accessed December 12, 2016, https://www.blueletterbible.org/lang/lexicon/lexicon .cfm?Strongs=G4151&t=KJV; Blue Letter Bible, s.v. "*ruwach*," accessed December 12, 2016, https://www.blueletterbible.org /lang/lexicon/lexicon.cfm?Strongs–H7307&t=KJV; Blue Letter Bible, s.v. "*nĕshamah*," accessed December 12, 2016, https://www .blueletterbible.org/lang/lexicon/lexicon.cfm?Strongs=H5397&t =KJV.

2. *Merrium-Webster*, s.v. "inspire," accessed December 12, 2016, http://www.merriam-webster.com/dictionary/inspire.

3. Francis Thompson, "The Hound of Heaven," *The Oxford Book of English Mystical Verse*, D. H. S. Nicholson and A. H. E. Lee, eds. (Oxford, England: Oxford University Press, 1917).

CHAPTER 4: THE HOLY SPIRIT AND POWER

1. Blue Letter Bible, s.v. "*en*," accessed December 13, 2016, https://www.blueletterbible.org/lang/lexicon/lexicon.cfm?Strongs =G1722&t=KJV.

2. F. F. Bosworth, *Christ the Healer* (Grand Rapids, MI: Chosen, 2008), 92.

3. "Seers Conference Thursday Night Session—12th May 2016," YouTube video, 7:00, Glory City Church, May 12, 2016, https://www.youtube.com/watch?v=f7vCrOHxtS8&feature =youtu.be&t=7m00s.

CHAPTER 6: THE COMFORT AND COUNSEL OF THE SPIRIT

1. Blue Letter Bible, s.v. *"epiriptō,"* accessed December 15, 2016, https://www.blueletterbible.org/lang/lexicon/lexicon.cfm ?Strongs=G1977&t=KJV.

CHAPTER 9: THE SPIRIT OF SUPERNATURAL PEACE

1. "Our Daughter's Heart Stopped, Then Jesus Walked In," September 23, 2016, accessed December 22, 2016, viewed at https://www.youtube.com/watch?v=y6uXGwO8lO8.

2. "The Moravians and John Wesley," *Christian History,* 1982, accessed October 13, 2016, http://www.christianitytoday .com/history/issues/issue-1/moravians-and-john-wesley.html.

CHAPTER 10: THE SPIRIT OF INTERCESSION

1. Jackie Pullinger and Andrew Quicke, *Chasing the Dragon* (Bloomington, Minnesota: Chosen Books, 1980), 85.

2. Ibid., 299–300.

CHAPTER 11: THE SPIRIT OF LOVE

1. Rick Howard and Jamie Lash, *This Was Your Life! Preparing to Meet God Face to Face* (Grand Rapids, MI: Chosen, 1998), 85.

2. Kriss Vallotton and Bill Johnson, *The Supernatural Ways of Royalty: Discovering Your Rights and Privileges of Being a Son or Daughter of God* (Shippensburg, PA: Destiny Image, 2006).

3. Pamela Rosewell Moore, *The Five Silent Years of Corrie Ten Boom* (Grand Rapids, MI: Zondervan, 1986), 92.

CHAPTER 12: YOUR CLOSEST FRIEND

1. Roberts Liardon, *Kathryn Kuhlman: A Spiritual Biography* (New Kensington, PA: Whitaker House, 2005).

2. Paul Simon (1966). "The 59th Street Bridge Song (Feelin' Groovy)," recorded by Simon & Garfunkel on *Parsley, Sage, Rosemary and Thyme* [LP].

3. Blue Letter Bible, s.v. *"damam,"* accessed December 22, 2016, https://www.blueletterbible.org/lang/lexicon/lexicon .cfm?Strongs=H1826&t=KJV.

ABOUT THE AUTHOR

KATHERINE RUONALA IS an author, evangelist, and conference speaker who carries a strong prophetic and healing anointing and witnesses many remarkable miracles in her meetings. Her message of the cross of Christ and His love, power, redemption, and grace reaches across denominational walls and has taken her to many nations around the world. Many are saved, healed, and delivered in her meetings, and her passion is to see people reconciled to God.

Katherine and her husband, Tom, are the senior ministers of Glory City Church, a multicampus church in Brisbane, Australia, and the overseers of the Glory City Church Network (GCN), which has churches and church plants throughout Australia and the United States. (Find more info at www.glorycitychurch.com.au.) She also hosts her own television program, *Glory City TV*, and has made appearances on Sid Roth's *It's Supernatural!* and CBN's *The 700 Club*. Katherine is also the founder and facilitator of the Australian Prophetic Council. She regularly travels and ministers at conferences around the world. Katherine and Tom are happily married and have three beautiful children, Jessica, Emily, and Joseph.

To contact Katherine Ruonala Ministries or to invite Katherine to minister, please go to http://www.katherineruonala.com/invitations/ or www.katherineruonala.com.

You may also write to Katherine Ruonala Ministries:

P.O. Box 1077

Springwood, Qld

Australia, 4127

For information on Glory City Church International Network or Glory City Church, visit www.glorycity church.com.au. To view live-streaming or video archives of Katherine's services, please see Glory City Church's YouTube channel at www.youtube.com/glorygathering.

To watch Glory City TV, visit www.glorycity.tv.

To partner with Katherine Ruonala ministries to take the Gospel of Salvation to the world, please visit http://www .katherineruonala.com/partnership/. To purchase additional Katherine Ruonala and Glory City Church resources, visit http://www.katherineruonala.com/resources/.